A Podenco's Tale

David Charles

Copyright © David Charles 2015

The right of David Charles to be identified as the author of this work has been asserted by him in accordance with the Copyright, Designs and patents Act 2015.

All rights reserved. No part of this publication may be reproduced, stored in or introduced into a retrieval system, or transmitted, in any form, or by any means (electronic, mechanical, photocopying, recording or otherwise) without the prior written permission of the author.
Any person who commits any unauthorised act in relation to this publication may be liable to criminal prosecution and civil claims for damages.

Also by David Charles

The House of Dreams
Black Eyes and Shattered Glass

David Charles lives for most of the year in southern Spain, with his wife Christine, two dogs and three cats. Born in Ipswich Suffolk, he started his own window cleaning business when he was twelve in order to earn pocket money and later took on a variety of jobs to pay his way through college. After college he worked in the telecommunications business for thirty five years reaching the level of senior manager in a multi-national telecommunications company.

His literary career began when he took early retirement. To date he has completed two books, 'The house of dreams' which was first published in October 2012 and ´Black eyes and shattered glass´ published in January 2015. He has also had a selection of poetry published in two anthologies and has written and delivered a one hour lecture on the life and career of Earl Kitchener of Khartoum.

Retirement gave him the opportunity to devote more time to his other hobbies which are reading, drawing, football and studying the people and events of the two world wars.

David has two sons, and two grandchildren.

This book is dedicated to man's best friend in general, and to my own four legged family in particular.

Me (beautiful and intelligent)

Prologue

Let me introduce myself, my name is Poppy and I am a Podenco. How I acquired my name is of no consequence at this stage, all will be revealed on that subject in due course. What we need to concentrate on at this point is the Podenco bit.

So what is a Podenco I hear you ask? A Podenco is a Spanish hunting dog used mainly in the hunting of rabbits and small mammals. I, however, am no ordinary Podenco. I am a Podenco Andaluz, which means that my strain is mainly to be found in the Andalucia region of Spain.

As an Andaluz I am one of the most intelligent and swiftest dogs around, and may I say, one of the most beautiful you will ever encounter. I have ears that stand proud like those of the Pharaoh hound, from whom I am directly descended. I have long slender legs that any model would be proud of, a barrel chest and a slim waist. I have a beautiful temperament and am faithful to a fault. In my opinion I am the queen of dogs.

I have had a very unusual life up until now and I thought you might like to read about it, so I persuaded

David, my pet human, to put it in print for me. I very much hope that you get as much enjoyment from reading my unique story as I have had dictating it.

Before you start reading, however, I just want to let you into an extremely well kept secret. We animals can talk to each other without humans detecting a sound. We can have complex conversations and are capable of intricate thought without you being aware at all. We have emotions too, we love, we hate, we smile, we frown, we feel fear, we feel happiness, we laugh and we cry. We don't have tear ducts so we cannot shed tears, but believe me we cry inside.

So you see we are not dumb animals, in fact in my experience no animal is dumb. Apart from the odd human that is.

oooOooo

I was born on April the first but as you will discover I was no April fool. The year was 2009 and the place, an old outhouse, that had definitely seen better days, and which formed part of a finca, or farmhouse, in the Axarquia region of Andalusia in southern Spain. Many decades previously some poor dirt farmer had scavenged rocks from the mountainside and crudely cemented them together with a primitive form of mortar to form the rough stone walls. Only now the cool wind would whistle through gaps that had been left as the ancient mortar crumbled and fell away. The roof beams had, long ago, been spindly olive trees and now provided food for the woodworm. They sagged under the weight of the chipped and cracked rustic tiles that channelled the winter rainwater into the yard beyond. Here and there were spaces where tiles were missing or broken and, during a downpour, if you were not careful where you lie, you could get a thorough soaking. The door was too short for the opening, because the bottom had rotted away, leaving a gap that scuttling rats would hurry through in order to steal some scraps of our food. The floor consisted of dirt mixed with generations of detritus and chicken droppings crushed into a firm warm tilth by thousands of footsteps.

This then was the sight that greeted me when I first opened my eyes to the world; this was to be my world. The dogs called it 'the shed'.

I shared the shed with my mother, three siblings, and five adult dogs. All of the adults had a hefty slice of Podenco in them, mixed over the generations with other various breeds which gave them a diverse ancestry. I, on the other hand, was pure Podenco Andaluz, as of course was my mother. I never discovered who my father was and I don't think my mother had much idea either. Whoever he was one thing was for sure, he was definitely pure Podenco too. He was probably a member of another hunter's pack who took a few minutes out from hunting one day, when the hunters were not looking, to have himself a little fun. The Podenco in us made everyone in the pack a natural hunter.

For now, along with my siblings, I lie snuggled to my mother's soft teat, drinking the milk that would one day make me big and strong. I looked up at mother, she was a small dog compared to most of the others, sable and white in colour with the gathering grey of age. She had the sagging teats that only half filled with milk which bore testament to the fact that we were the most recent of many litters. Her eyes looked rheumy as she gazed lovingly on us. She was thin, painfully thin, underfed and tired. Dispirited she just lie there and nuzzled us to her warm belly.

As I grew during those early weeks I would rough and tumble with my brothers, I was the only female of the litter, and gradually my muscles became strong. Life for me was one round of suckling, wrestling and sleeping, innocently I thought this was all life would consist of. I said to myself 'life is great'.

Life stayed great, or to be more accurate I stayed innocent, right up to the day when the hunting season started and the human came. I heard heavy footfalls approaching followed by a scraping sound as the latch was worked. This had happened every day and was usually followed with a bucket load of scraps tipped onto the floor for the adults to eat. Not so this time, all the adults sensed the difference and began to bark wildly, jumping up at the door. All, that is, except mother.

The door was flung open and there stood a stocky human wearing patched brown trousers and a thick cotton shirt. I hadn't really studied him before, thinking he was just someone who brought food, but today I eyed him carefully. His face was tanned brown and leathery, his hair was unkempt and he obviously hadn't shaved for a few days. In the middle of his craggy face was a bulbous, rosy nose that betrayed heavy drinking. It was the first time I had noticed his eyes, they were dark and cold, too small for his face really, a shiver ran down my back.

The human rounded up the adult dogs and encouraged them out of the doorway with a rough kick or two from his thick leather boots.

"I'll leave the old bitch here with the new ones," he mumbled to himself as he cast a look over his shoulder at mother, "she won't be much use to me today."

Outside in the yard the dogs bayed excitedly. The wooden door slammed shut, there was the grinding sound of the latch sliding into place and the shed fell suddenly silent. Not so outside, the dogs were getting more and more excited, so I rushed over to the door and poked my snout through the gap below the dry rotted boards to see what all the excitement was about. I realised that this was actually the first time I had seen the world beyond the shed door and my first impression was that it was huge and strange. My attention immediately went to a battered old four by four with a small square box trailer hooked onto the back. The human was driving the yapping dogs into the trailer. One was a bit slow at getting in and was grabbed roughly by the scruff of the neck and thrown carelessly on top of the others.

When the last dog was in the human slammed a metal grille over the opening and climbed into the car. The dogs continued their wild barking as the human crunched into first gear, dropped the clutch and they all disappeared in a cloud of dust, out through a gap in the stone wall, and were gone.

As the billows of dust began to settle, and the baying of the dogs grew fainter, I had my first real look around at what lie outside. There was a big stone built farmhouse that had definitely seen better days. It had patches in the walls, where rocks had become dislodged and been roughly repaired with cement. Where the holes had been too big there were two or three bricks rudely cemented into place to make a running repair and clumps of bushy green weed sprang from many of the mortar gaps, giving the impression of continued decay. Cut into the wall was a big wooden door with dark green paint that was blistered and peeling, either side of the door were two small windows with rough wooden shutters that hung at odd angles.

Six wooden beams were lodged into the wall, supported at their outward end by rustic brick pillars. Over these beams grew an ancient gnarled grape vine forming a canopy that provided shelter from the hot summer sun. Underneath there stood a long wooden table with a couple of benches and some chairs where the humans would sit in the warm summer evenings to eat their food and guzzle their wine. The yard itself was rough dirt with sprigs of vegetation along the base of the walls, and a plethora of old rusting farm implements, abandoned where they had last fallen. Strewn amongst these was a clutch of discarded earthenware jugs. A few scraggy chickens poked and prodded their worn beaks at the gritty ground searching for any hidden morsels of food.

I pulled my snout back from under the door and turned to mother.

"Where are they going?" I asked.

"They are going hunting." She explained.

"Hunting? What is that?"

"Well," she began, "the human takes us to the campo, that's the countryside, and lets us out of the trailer. We search around until we sniff out where the rabbits are and then we chase them. Sometimes we catch one and take it back to the human and sometimes they shoot it while we are chasing it. Either way they bring them home for food."

"That sounds like fun, but..." I hesitated.

"What is it dear?"

"What is a rabbit?" I asked shyly. She chuckled lovingly and described for me what a rabbit looked like.

"Don't worry though," she smiled. "You will know one when you see one, your instincts will tell you."

"So why are we all left here? Why haven't we gone hunting with everybody else?"

"I'm afraid you four are much too young to go as yet but when you are a little older the human will take you with him."

"And you'll be with us won't you mum?"

"I doubt it dear; I'm getting too old for all that running about. Anyway by then I might have some new puppies to look after."

Was that all she existed for, I thought to myself, litter after litter, how boring her life must be.

As the sun began to slide down the sky and the heat of the day eased I heard the car again. I slid across to the door and shoved my snout into the warm dry air eager to witness their return. The aged four by four swept into the yard, throwing a shower of stones and dust into the air, and slid to a halt in front of the sun canopy. The human got out, opened the rear door and dragged out a bunch of furry brown objects, which I instantly recognised as the rabbit creatures that mother had described to me. Slinging them casually over his shoulder he strode off into the farmhouse, emerging a few minutes later he walked to the rear of the trailer and prised open the metal grille allowing the dogs to spill out into the yard. They followed him as he came over to the shed, worked the latch and kicked open the door. I only just moved out of the way in time to avoid receiving what would have been a nasty bang on the head from the swinging door. Exhausted from their exploits, the dogs lumbered into the shed and flopped onto the floor, panting deeply with their tongues lolling limply from the sides of their mouths and dripping saliva.

That must be great, I said to myself, I was impatient to join in and do some hunting of my own; I couldn't wait to be older.

Later that evening the human returned to the shed and tossed a bucket load of scraps into the middle of the floor. The adult dogs fell on the fare ravenously. A couple of scuffles broke out as one or two got more than their share, but within a minute it was all gone. I noticed that mum didn't get any.

The days raced by and my brothers and I were growing fast. We were soon off mother's milk and found that we too had to scramble for a share of the food that the human threw into the shed. This was when I learnt a very important lesson. In my naivety I had not noticed, and it had not occurred to me, that there was a hierarchy within the shed. The first time I made a move toward the food I received a painful head butt to my ribs from 'Big Blackie', so called because he was just that, big and black. He had dark soulless eyes set in a broad head and was the undisputed boss of the pack.

"Wait your turn runt." He growled at me as I shrank away from him. "We have been working while you pups have been playing games so you eat last."

With that he pushed me to one side and proceeded to tuck into the food. The other adults joined him but I noticed that one of the others, the one with a chewed up ear, who went by the name of 'Earhole' winked at me as he moved to take up his share. My brothers and I waited until the adults had their fill before we tentatively descended on the meagre remnants.

Later that night Earhole sidled over to me and whispered that I needed to be a bit more careful.

"Big Blackie is the leader of the pack." He explained. "You ought to try not to upset him. What he says goes until he leaves the pack or until someone is strong enough to take the leadership from him. I challenged him once." His head drooped as he remembered the contest. "Look what he did to my ear. Nearly chewed it right off."

"Thank you, I will be more careful in future, I don't want to end up with an ear like yours." He smiled at my cheeky remark. I was silent in thought for a while then plucked up courage to ask him. "Do you enjoy hunting?"

"Mmm I suppose so, never really thought about it. It's just what we have to do. I suppose it beats lying here all the time like your mother."

"What is it like to hunt?" I asked excitedly.

"Well little one." He began. "It's not all it's cracked up to be; not all fun and frolics. It is usually extremely hard work. We have to run around all over the mountain searching for the scent of a rabbit and when we find the spoor we have to flush him out, because they invariably hide at first, then we have to chase and catch him. They aren't anywhere near as quick as us, and they are usually stupid, so most times that bit isn't too difficult."

He had my full attention; I was really excited, keen to have a go myself.

"That sounds easy." I said naively.

"They jink around as they run away from us, constantly changing their direction," he continued, "because they think that they can turn quicker than us and they can give us the slip, which they sometimes do, but not often. We pay no mind to that jinking stuff and run fairly straight."

I was enthralled.

"But if they change direction and you don't doesn't that mean that you can lose them?" I thought I was being clever now.

"No girl, you see, every time they jink they lose a bit of ground but they usually head in the same general direction, by running a straighter line than them we can gain ground, after a while, we get close enough to jump on them and kill them. The secret is to read their intentions, second guess them. They run to a pattern and when you recognise that pattern you have it cracked. Knowing exactly when to jump is important too, jump too soon and he might get away."

That night I curled up to sleep with all Earhole had said running through my head. I dreamed that I was chasing a rabbit round the yard. I was excited to become a hunter; I wanted to be the best hunter that the human had ever had.

I spent most evenings sitting with Earhole listening intently to the tales he had to tell about the hunts he had been on in the past, firing questions at him until, by the time I was about three months old, I knew all there was to know about hunting. At least I thought I did, unfortunately I only knew the good bits.

Apart from Big Blackie and Earhole there were three other adult dogs in the shed. There was ´White tail´, named for obvious reasons, ´Paws´, who had enormous feet for his size and 'Dozy', who seemed to spend most of his life asleep. Paws, White Tail and Dozy were only about a year older than me but Big Blackie and Earhole were veterans at about three years old.

Each time they returned from a hunting expedition the two elderly statesmen would laze around; whereas the others would have a short lie down to recover their strength before becoming restless and stalking around the shed. All except Dozy that is, who just slept and slept.

As we grew older feeding time became more competitive amongst me and my siblings, we waited until the adults had their fill and as soon as they moved away we would dive in. I used to push to get as much food as I could with scant regard for anybody else, I was determined to be big and strong, but, looking back now I feel a bit guilty because I realise that the one amongst us who got very little food, the one that I deprived more than most, was mother.

We pups were independent of mother now and in our haste to grow big and strong we kind of neglected her. She would lie quietly in a corner of the shed just watching with her sad, tired eyes.

Early one morning the human burst into the shed with a length of rope in his hand, I remember thinking it was strange because it was not a hunting day. He waded through the throng of dogs, yapping expectantly round his ankles, went up to mother and tied the rope loosely around her neck. She cast a knowing look toward me and my brothers before, with a sharp tug on the rope, he led her out of the shed.

As the door slammed, and the latch grated into place, I skidded across the floor and thrust my snout through the gap to see where he was taking her.

She had an air of sadness about her as she was ushered across the yard, her head bowed low with her tail hanging listlessly between her haunches, she plodded with a slow, exhausted gait.

"Where are you going mother?" I whimpered under the door. Slowly she turned her head and fixed me with her baleful brown eyes.

"You be a good girl now, don't you worry yourself about me." She whispered, and with that she turned and trudged beside the human, through the gate and was lost to my view. I stayed with my snout pushed firmly into the hole determined to be the first to welcome her on her return, all to no avail. That was the last time I ever saw my mother, for when the human returned the end of the rope that had been tied around her neck, was dragging unceremoniously in the dirt.

Now that my brothers and I were on our own we had to look to the other adults for comfort and advice. I became firm friends with Earhole, he was always so laid back and friendly. He christened me 'Girl', a name that stuck with me. I think he was secretly pleased that Big Blacky had taken leadership of the pack because he really wasn't the forceful type, he was far too gentle, far too sensitive, anyway he preferred to be one of the boys. He confided to me that he thought the younger adults were too boisterous and full of their own importance, even Dozy when he was awake, so under his guidance I kept a discrete distance from them.

Almost as soon as mother disappeared our lives changed drastically and forever. The time had arrived for us to learn our trade, no longer were we to be treated as puppies, we were working dogs and we would have to earn our keep, so when the day arrived for the next hunt we were taken along too. The human strode into the shed and chased us out toward the trailer, giving a painful helping boot up the tail if we were too slow.

When I reached the trailer it occurred to me that I hadn't taken too much notice of it up until then, but when I looked into the back of it I became very anxious, even afraid. It was very small and claustrophobic. I didn´t want to get in. Constructed completely of metal with no ventilation, save for a couple of holes at the front and the removable grille at the back, it looked daunting. Nine of us would never fit in there I thought. I stopped and looked at my brothers.

I'm not going in there!

The human did not hear me.

"I'm not going in there." I said to the other dogs and I stood my ground. That was when I learned my first painful lesson of the day. I heard a loud thwack and felt a terrific pain in my back. Turning my head I saw the human standing there, glaring at me, his face like thunder. Poised above his head was a thick wooden stick that had been the source of my pain. I was transfixed; motionless. As a result I learned painful lesson number two, which was to move more quickly. I didn't, and his arm swung again, the stick swished through the air and landed with a whack across my hind quarters, he wielded it with reckless abandon. I snarled at him. I bared my teeth. As if by magic, Earhole was by my side.

"Just get into the trailer Girl, quickly." He said with urgency in his voice. "Don't make him angry or he'll hurt you even more." With that he nuzzled me toward the back of the trailer.

"He has already hurt me." I whimpered as we made to climb in.

"That's nothing; trust me. If you don't obey him straight away he will *really* hurt you. Come on." With that he hopped in.

I was not quick enough and I felt a big hand grab me roughly by the scruff of the neck, I couldn't feel ground under my paws, I was dangling. Viciously he aimed me in the general direction of the trailer.

"I said get in." He rasped. "I can see I'm going to have trouble with you."

I bounced painfully off the hard metal floor and my muzzle slammed into the front wall. My nose stung with the pain. My brothers followed me into the trailer, needing surprisingly little persuasion. We were all in a tangle, legs everywhere, and as we rolled about trying to regain our feet the adult dogs flew into the trailer, under their own steam, and landed on top of us. There was definitely not enough room, it was not designed to hold nine dogs, even though four of us were much smaller than the others, there was hardly any room to move. Last to enter the trailer was Big Blackie. He hopped sedately in with a superior look on his face.

"Sort yourselves out." He boomed as he looked down his snout at us. "Move out of my way. You little ones get to the front, I want my space."

Sheepishly we did as he told us.

The four by four lurched forward and set off at what seemed a break neck speed, the trailer bouncing remorselessly over the rough stony track. Taken by surprise my brothers and I were thrown around in the dark recesses at the front of the trailer.

Big Blackie, on the other hand, had pride of place by the grille so he was able to get plenty of fresh air, unlike the rest of us. He didn't even look in our direction he just kept his upper class snout pointed arrogantly upward.

Earhole elbowed his way through the mass of hot canine flesh to the front of the trailer where I was sitting on a very sore rump.

"You must never do that again Girl." He whispered with concern in his voice. "You must never ever try and defy the will of the human. He sees us as tools to help him catch rabbits and if any one of us causes trouble for him they are beaten with that stick and sometimes he takes it out on the rest of us just for good measure. I remember there was one who constantly defied him and he disappeared, never to return. So please, for our sakes as well as your own, don't make trouble. OK."

"What about mother?" I asked. "She never caused any trouble but she has disappeared."

"Yes and I'm afraid she won't be coming back either."

"So why did she go away?"

"She was only wanted for breeding, her whole purpose in life was to give birth to litter after litter of hunting dogs."

"So why did she go away then?" I repeated.

"She was getting too old and weak; she couldn't have any more strong dogs, and besides you came along, Girl."

"I came along? What's that got to do with it?"

"Haven't you realised yet?" He looked at me as if I ought to know what he was about to say. "Do I really have to spell it out?" My look obviously told him that he did.

"All the other puppies are male. The human needed a strong, young female to take over the breeding from your mother." He paused. "You are that young female. That will be your place in the future of the pack. You will provide the next few generations of puppies."

"You mean that I will be a puppy machine for the rest of my life?"

"Exactly! Just as soon as you are old enough and can demonstrate to him that you have the hunting instinct in you."

I slumped to the floor, I was desolate and frightened. I remembered mother's worn out gaze, the look of devastation in her tired eyes and her sagging loose body. That was what he had in store for me? No way! Absolutely not! Not if I had anything to do with it.

The car bounced noisily along the rough track, up steep hills, down steep hills, round tight bends, all the way followed by a billowing cloud of dry brown powdery dust. Suddenly, the human hit the brakes and, with a jolt, we slid to a halt. After the manic drive the silence was deafening, punctuated only by the ticking of the car engine as it cooled. The dust slowly began to settle behind us. The adult dogs began to bark excitedly, clamouring, pawing at the grille eager to escape the trailer, all too aware of what lie ahead. It seemed an age but eventually the human slipped the latch, removed the grille, and allowed the occupants to spill onto the dusty hillside.

I stood spellbound as I took in the stark rocky landscape. I could see hills, mountains, trees, sky and clouds. A voice beside me knocked me from my reverie.

"Stick with me, I'll show you what to do." As ever it was the faithful Earhole.

The human shouted commands that I didn't understand and all the adult dogs shot off in different directions. I saw the tail of Earhole disappearing into the dry standing grass. Spurred into action I quickly followed lest I lose sight of him, he may have been older but he was certainly fast. It only took a few minutes before there was excited barking behind us. I stopped, looking over my shoulder to see what all the fuss was about I spied Paws, chasing down a rabbit. The rabbit jinked this way and that, trying to throw the experienced chaser off its tail, but he seemed to be able to anticipate each move and managed to cut the corners so that he gained an important metre every time. I was transfixed. Closer and closer he got until there seemed to be no distance between them. Paws leapt, grabbing the rabbit as he flew over him, and they hit the ground in a flurry of fur and dust. Immediately Paws clamped his jaws around the rabbit's chest and squeezed the life out of him. It was all over in a few seconds.

Proudly he picked up the lifeless form, which drooped loosely either side of his powerful jaws, and with head held high he pranced over to the waiting human.

"That's how it's done girl." Earhole gave me a wry smile. "C'mon, we had better find one of our own." Five minutes later Earhole paused and snuffled the ground, he had detected the scent of his quarry.

"There's a rabbit nearby," he whispered, "stay close to me and run when I run." Slowly he crept forward with his nose perilously close to the ground. The rabbit was hiding, pressed into the vegetation somewhere ahead of us, trying to make himself invisible. Closer and closer crept Earhole until the rabbit could resist his instincts no longer. He panicked. Realising that he was about to be discovered he decided to take his chance and make a bolt for it. Up he sprang and off he sped, little white tail flashing as his hind legs kicked him on. Earhole made after him.

"There he goes girl. Follow me." His words were whipped away on the breeze as he charged, full speed, after the doomed rabbit. I bounded after them both, watching carefully as the rabbit regularly changed direction, instinct driven by panic. Not so Earhole, he seemed to know where the rabbit was headed and when it would turn, he cut the corner every time it veered off at an angle. Over the hill we went, down a hollow, round a bush, leaping over rocks gaining ground all the time. Earhole was just a metre behind his quarry now and the rabbit turned his head to see where his pursuer was.

That was a fatal mistake. His look cost him vital speed and with it his life, that was all Earhole needed. He pounced and his claws caught the rabbit on his hips. The sudden extra weight made his hind legs buckle and they tumbled together in a cloud of dust. The breeze dispersed the dust cloud quickly and I saw the frightened rabbit's eyes bulge as Earhole clamped his powerful jaws around his chest. His mouth opened in silent complaint and his tongue lolled out as he felt his life breath being denied him. A couple of convulsions and it was all over. The rabbit lie lifeless before us.

"You take it back to the human, Girl, I'll see if I can find another one." With that he was gone, snout almost scraping the dust as he stalked his way over the hillside.

I looked down at the twisted fur in front of me. It was so sad, only moments before this had been an innocent rabbit, happily going about his life but now; now it was just a lump of fur covered meat. The eyes, so recently bright, were already beginning to dull and the twinkle was drying to opacity. I felt elation at the kill but also sympathy and sadness for the unfortunate creature. Slowly I grabbed it, hoisted it into my mouth, the way I had seen Paws do a few minutes earlier, and proudly made my way back to the human.

I expected that he would be pleased to see me and that my prize would lead to some sort of praise but I was to be severely disappointed. I trotted, rather ungainly with my awkward load, up to the human standing in front of a small pile of rabbits. I dropped my catch at his feet and looked up at him expectantly.

"Don't just sit there, go get another." He growled, giving me a sharp kick in the ribs with his heavy boot. That hurt. I scurried away searching once more for Earhole. I was beginning to dislike this human with a vengeance; all he seemed to understand was how to inflict pain; were all humans like this I asked myself.

I didn't actually catch anything myself that day, in truth my prize really belonged to Earhole, but I had learned a few valuable lessons.

Back at the shed I sidled off into a corner, away from everybody else, and curled into a ball, my ribs were bruised but not as much as my pride. I ruminated on the events of the morning. In my mind I relived the elation of the chase, the sadness at the death of the rabbit and felt anger at the pain in my back, rump and ribs. Most of all I felt a deep depression creeping over me as I contemplated the life that was mapped out ahead of me. If Earhole was correct, and I had no reason to doubt his word, the hunt would soon be a thing of the past for me.

Today I had enjoyed the freedom to run, the open air, the sun on my back, the thrill of the hunt, the ecstasy of success. I didn't want to spend my life closeted away in this shed having brood after brood of puppies, turning my body into a flaccid milk machine. I didn't want the life mother had endured but what could I do to prevent it? I felt trapped.

The following week we went hunting again and I recollected the painful lessons I had learnt the last time. When the human came to rouse us I didn't put up any resistance, I resolved to be at the front of the pack, well away from the stick and the boot. I could still feel the tenderness in my ribs and back. Quickly I jumped into the trailer, closely followed by the others. I made my way to the front corner and lie down. Last in, as usual, was Big Blackie who hopped arrogantly onto the space that everybody had left vacant by the grille. He surveyed the trailer to make sure we were all in our correct places and that we had left him sufficient room, before stretching out across the trailer so that he alone could enjoy all the fresh air.

Arriving at the hunting ground there was the usual clamouring to escape the stifling heat of the trailer and exchange its hot stuffiness for the warm sweetness of fresh air. I had decided that this time I would try hunting on my own, without the aid of Earhole. I was desperate to make a good impression. I thought maybe if I was a really good hunter I just might not end up as the litter bin. On the human's command I trotted off across the coarse dry landscape with my nose close to the ground eagerly searching for that distinctive scent. Minutes passed and I had detected nothing. Then there was a sharp bark, one of the others had picked up a trail and was running the rabbit to ground. Almost immediately there was another bark, then another and another, they were all picking up scents and chasing their quarry. Still I found nothing, I began to panic, my scheme was beginning to unravel before it had even started. On and on I searched with no luck whatsoever until it was time for the troop to return to the farm.

There was quite a haul from the other dogs and there were even two rabbits that the human had shot with his rifle. At the time the crack of the shot had surprised me, it was the first time I had seen or heard, a rifle being fired.

"You're a total waste of space today." Grumbled the human as I approached, my head bowed in apology. "Didn't even get a whiff did ya?" His boot propelled me into the trailer.

"Don't know why he brings you with us." Moaned Big Blackie. "You should be back at the shed rearing some new broods."

"She can't yet you fool." Piped in Earhole. Big Blackie bristled with indignation; nobody spoke to him in that tone. He glared at Earhole. Unperturbed Earhole continued. "She's not old enough to have a litter until she's over six months; I thought you of all hounds would know that." Big Blackie narrowed his eyes in temper. He would store that insult up for later.

"Can't happen soon enough." He grumbled, lifting his nose in the air as if he'd picked up a nasty smell. He turned to face the grille. Twice during the journey he flashed a look of pure vitriol in Earhole's direction. It was returned with a confident smirk.

I was not the only one who suffered a lack of success that day, Dozy seemed to have lost his edge too. Apparently he hadn't caught a rabbit in three weeks. While all the other dogs had been busy catching rabbits we were both perceived as failures, aimlessly scurrying over the landscape. On the subsequent hunt the situation didn't improve either, both me and Dozy came up blank again, search as we may it seemed that we were always destined to be in the wrong place at the wrong time. The human was getting impatient with us, moaning continually to himself, as he herded the pack into the trailer.

"Thank god it won't be long before she starts breeding. That other hasn't got what it takes either. Waste of good food. I'll give them one last try next week."

That didn't sound like good news for either of us. I would be stuck in the shed shelling out puppies by the dozen and presumably Dozy would be left there with me. I was soon to discover how wrong I was.

The following hunt we were all sent off on a search and fortunately for me I caught a scent early on. I crept along the spoor watching carefully for the tell tale movement that would herald the chase as the rabbit made his final desperate run for freedom. A few metres ahead of me I detected a small twitch in the bush, instinctively I knew it was not the breeze, at long last I had my very own target very close.

I crept cautiously forward. There was a sudden swish of vegetation and the flash of a white tail, he had broken cover and was off and running. Remembering all that Earhole had taught me, I bounded after the furry flier. He jinked right, I veered slightly. He jinked left, right back into my path. Gradually I closed on him. Distantly I heard Earhole shouting encouragement to me. The rabbit jinked left again before making a sweeping turn to the right, I cut inside him, rapidly shortening the distance between us. I was now only a metre behind him. The climax of the chase, I had him. I leapt. I came crashing down expecting to feel his warm furriness beneath me, but all I felt was stony ground. Quickly I looked around, somehow I had missed him, his flashing white tail disappeared over a rise and he was gone, too far away now for me to renew the chase. Miserably I realised that my exuberance and over confidence had got the better of me, I had leapt just that important split second too soon, something that Earhole had warned me about. I had lost impetus in the air, not much but, sufficient for him to open the gap and escape. I would not make that mistake again, assuming that I got another chance that was.

I could almost feel the groan of disappointment from Earhole and as I turned to look back he stared straight at me.

"Don't be downhearted Girl." He encouraged. "Sometimes that happens. Get out there and find another trail quickly."

Disconsolately I pawed the ground and made my way back toward the spot where I had first picked up the scent. I circled around the area until I picked up a new trail. I could hardly believe my luck, two spoors within minutes of each other. Carefully I stalked the trail, all the time the scent was getting noticeably stronger. I was determined that I would run this target down but could detect no movement in the vegetation ahead of me. This rabbit was playing it very cool, this one obviously thought he could wait me out and that I would pass him by. I poked my nose under a bush, the trail became extremely strong, I nuzzled the fronds of the bush aside and found myself staring full into the frightened beady eyes of the biggest rabbit I had ever seen.

For a fraction of a second we both stared at each other, frozen by the surprise, then he jumped high in the air, twisted, landed and bolted all in one continuous, smooth movement.

It took me half a second to recover from the shock before I was up and bounding after him. I held my head low, straining every muscle and sinew to extract every ounce of speed that I could. With almost every stride he jinked right or left desperately trying to wrong foot me. I remembered all the advice Earhole had imparted to me and I forced myself to keep an almost straight line. I guessed the rabbit was an old timer because, although he changed direction rapidly and regularly, his overall speed was noticeably slower than the previous rabbit had been, he seemed to be tiring. With every jink I gained valuable centimetres on him so that I slowly began to overhaul him.

Determination set in, I was desperate not to make the same mistake again, I knew this could be my last chance, I must hold my nerve and not leap too soon. This old boy would pay the price for my education. Surely I was close enough but I wanted to be even closer. His bobbing white tail was almost touching my nose, just another couple of centimetres that's all I need. Now I realised that I didn't have to leap on him so in mid stride I swept my front paw sideways and felt it connect with his rear leg. His legs tangled and he lost his balance tumbling in a cloud of mountain dust. I was on him in a flash. My jaws engulfed his chest and I squeezed the life breath out of him. I kept squeezing until his eyes dulled and I knew I had done it. I had my first kill.

I stood over his inert form, mixed feelings flooding my mind. I had made my first kill and I was euphoric for that, but I had extinguished the life of another creature and for that I felt sad. Maybe I would have felt different if the kill was to enable me to feed myself, but it wasn't, the kill was simply to keep the human happy. If I'm honest it was also to prevent me getting another whack from that dreaded stick the human wielded with impunity. I had done it; I was now a qualified hunter.

The rabbit was very large and it was with extreme difficulty that I picked him up and struggled back towards the human. I tried to trot, the furry head swinging loosely on one side of my jaw and the hind legs dragging on the ground the other side, leaving two shallow furrows in the dust. My jaws ached so much that I had to put my prize down, once or twice, to relieve the growing numbness in my jaw muscles, eventually I arrived at the four by four with my burden and dropped it at the human's feet. Again I half expected some sort of accolade for my triumph, just a little word of praise, but once more I was to be disappointed, the human simply scraped it from the ground and cast it into the back of the car. The hunt was over for the day and I was ushered toward the trailer. He called in the rest of the pack.

Unfortunately Dozy had, once more, been unlucky, he had missed the trails yet again and had not picked up a single scent. I guessed that would mean that he would have to remain in the shed next time we hunted. All the dogs clustered around the trailer waiting their turn to jump in, all that is except Dozy. He was still frantically searching for a trail to follow, desperate for a rabbit to bring back. The trailer grille was closed.

Wait! You've forgotten Dozy. He is still out there searching.

The human didn't hear me.

"Dozy." I shouted. "Quickly come to the trailer, we're leaving."

I saw Dozy's head come off the ground and point in our direction, he had heard me and he realised that the grille had been closed with him on the wrong side of it. He stood rooted for a second just staring at the trailer before breaking into a run as panic began to set in. He headed directly toward us terrified that he might be left behind.

In desperation his speed picked up, ears flapping like sheets on a linen line, and he was now only ten metres from the trailer, surely the human must see him.

There was a crack and Dozy crumpled in a heap, tumbling head over heels before coming to rest in a cloud of light brown dust with red flecks in it. He lie there for a second, raised his head and fixed his uncomprehending, confused eyes on the trailer, his family and the human. Another crack rang out and the light went out of his eyes. Unconcerned the human climbed into the four by four, gunned the engine and headed for the farm.

There was an eerie, shocked silence in the trailer as we bounced our way home. When the grille was finally removed we crept silently away to the shed, all of us deep in thought.

As I lie on the floor of the shed that night I came to the realisation that we were all just lumps of meat to the human, lumps of meat that helped to fill his larder, other than that we were completely expendable. He held no feelings for us at all. I couldn't eat that night. I kept replaying in my mind what had happened, visions of Dozy kept coming into my head. Again I saw that look of panic on his face when he realised that the trailer was loaded, the fear that he might be left behind, his obvious and mounting relief as he raced across the scrub bringing him nearer and nearer to the trailer, his look of utter confusion as he crumpled into a heap, and that last second, when a mask of resignation and disbelief flashed onto his face as he finally realised he would not be travelling back with the rest of us.

I found it incredible that the human had just left him lying there, easy prey to the foxes, the rats and the buzzards that regularly circled the mountains.

Unable to sleep, I cried for Dozy most of the night.

The next day I began to think seriously about my own predicament. The Dozy episode and the way my own mother had disappeared constantly played on my mind. I was almost six months old and Earhole had told me that I was approaching the time when I would be taking up my position as a breeding machine. I desperately didn't want to be a litter factory, I enjoyed the freedom that existed in the mountains and I didn't want to give that freedom up. I would *not* give that freedom up. I had to do something about it and I had to do it soon. There seemed only one course of action open to me; I had to run away.

Over the next couple of days I formulated my plan.

Hunting day came around once more and I waited with some trepidation, would the human decide to leave me in the shed or would I go in the trailer with all the others. I had to be on the hunt or my plan would be doomed before it had even begun. My silent question was answered when the human strode across the yard and kicked open the shed door.

"C'mon you lot." He shouted. I jumped up with the others but made a conscious effort to keep myself hidden from his view, just in case seeing me might make him change his mind and leave me behind. I dropped my head and sidled between Earhole and White tail using them as cover. Together we trotted to the open trailer and clambered in. Swiftly I made my way to my usual front corner and curled up. The grille was locked on, the human climbed into the car, and we were off. So far so good, part one of the plan successfully completed.

When I clambered from the trailer I was shocked to see that this time the hunting ground was a different one, somewhere that we had never been to before. That threw my carefully formulated plan out of the window straight away. I had banked on us being on our usual killing field when I made my bid for freedom, I had planned to use a long depression in the landscape, one that had been eroded by eons of rainwater. I had calculated that I could slip into the channel whilst the human's attention was elsewhere and be well out of range long before he realised that I was missing.

I looked around and studied the new landscape. I knew I had to make my break today or not at all because I was certain that I would never get another chance. My only option was to use the terrain to my best advantage, I had no choice, I had to work with what I had available. I looked around, the landscape was barren, low shrubs that no doubt hid many rabbits but which offered no cover for me. My heart sank. We were on the side of a long sloping hillside, the only way out was over the top of the rise and the route was totally devoid of cover. I had to chance it, there was no other way I could go, I would need luck, and plenty of it, but my mind was made up.

Despite my concerns I tried to act as normally as I could, I had been second from last out of the trailer, again trying not to draw attention to myself, and gave the impression of searching for a scent along with everybody else. As I quartered the ground I gradually made my way up the hillside. I detected a presence behind me and turning found myself face to face with Earhole.

"What's going on?" He asked.

"What do you mean, what's going on?" I replied innocently.

"You are very much on edge today, you seem so highly strung. Some of the others have noticed it too. So?"

"So?"

"So what are you up to?" I realised that I had to tell him, he had been such a good friend to me.

"Oh Earhole, I'm so frightened." I could feel myself becoming emotional. "I don't want to become a litter machine. I don't want to spend the rest of my life in the shed pushing out puppies. I want to live, I want freedom."

"We would all like freedom Girl, we all dream about it, but you need to accept that's all it will ever be, a dream."

"Not for me." I said emphatically. "I refuse to be a litter machine."

"Unfortunately there isn't much you can do about it though is there."

"Yes there is, I'm going to run away." Earhole chuckled.

"Don't you think we've all dreamt of running away at one time or another Girl?"

"So why haven't you?"

"It's not as easy as it sounds. For one, it's much too dangerous. The human watches us closely all the time, you know that if we get too far away from him he calls us back. He knows we would love to be free but he can't afford to lose us, and especially he can't afford to lose you."

"Because of my breeding value?"

"Exactly. He will do anything to keep you, even if it means shooting you in the legs, and he will do just that, it's your belly he needs not your legs." Earhole had frightened me but I was still ready to risk it for freedom.

"I'll take my chances."

"Girl, think carefully, you could end up like Dozy."

"Or I could end up like mother, which is worse? I ask you which scenario is worse?"

"You are determined, aren't you?" He thought for a second. "So what is your plan, I presume you have one?"

"I will work my way up the hillside and get as far away from the human as I can, then when he is not looking I will make a break for it. If I can just get over the crest before he realises what I'm doing I will make it. I will be free."

"You make it sound very easy, but your chances of success are slim, you must be extremely careful. If he even suspects that you are going to do a runner he will cripple you. It's the way these humans are. If you don't play by their rules they take you out of the game." Earhole was obviously extremely concerned for me. "You are sure about this aren't you?" I nodded. "OK, give me a few minutes, I'll have a word with Paws and White Tail, they really like you, I'll see if we can do anything to help, cause a diversion or something. I can't promise anything." He paused. "Be lucky Girl." With that he rubbed his muzzle on my cheek.

"Thank you Earhole, you are a real friend." I nuzzled him and rubbed my snout along his neck. He licked my ear briefly and then he was gone.

I watched as he approached Paws and White tail, they cast a quick glance in my direction, then the three of them trotted off. I put my snout down as if searching for a scent and continued sweeping the hillside, slowly but surely working my way up the gradient.

I was about fifty metres from the crest when things started to unravel. The human noticed that I was wandering off too far and he shouted for me to come lower down the slope. Freedom was tantalisingly close, there was no way I was going back, I continued. I glanced down the slope, the human, still shouting at me, reached into the four by four and retrieved his rifle. That was my cue, I set off for the crest of the hill as fast as my legs would carry me.

He raised the rifle to his shoulder and I waited for the inevitable crack followed by a searing pain but it didn't come. Instead there was a tremendous commotion. Over my shoulder I saw Earhole and Paws charge toward the startled hunter while White Tail ran in circles round him, barking his head off. I saw the human turn on them in surprise, he lowered his rifle and shouted at them. As they ran close to him he lashed out with the rifle, using it as a club. Earhole took a painful blow to his ribs and in retaliation he jumped up at the human, teeth bared, receiving the butt to the side of his head for his pains. He fell with a sickening yelp. Determined to defend his friend Paws made a beeline for the human and ran straight into him, catching him knee high, the human cried out in pain and crumpled to the ground. I knew this was my only chance, the chance that my friends had sacrificed so much to give me, straining every muscle I increased my speed and made directly for the summit.

The human, still on the ground rubbing his damaged knee, turned his attention to me once more and lifting his rifle to his shoulder swung round to take a bead on me. I plunged through a patch of dry scratchy brush, running for my very life. I heard a crack and saw a puff of dust a couple of centimetres to my left, he was a good shot. Almost there. Another crack, another puff of dust just at the moment I reached the crest. I dived for the far side, and safety, as another crack rang out, this time I saw no puff of dust.

I had done it. Well I had done the hard part anyway, I was out of sight of the human and my friends had made sure that he could not come after me, not with that injured knee. Thanks to my friends I had a good start. I paused momentarily for breath, I knew they would suffer retribution, I hoped they would be alright. I had to make a success of my freedom, for them.

"Thanks guys, all the best to you."

There was another crack. I was confused; the human was not in sight so he could not be shooting at me. I turned my back on the hunt and ploughed on. I ran and ran and ran until I could run no more. It seemed as if I had been running for hours, the sky was darkening, night was coming, I collapsed under a bush, totally exhausted, and lie there panting heavily. Every muscle ached, my tongue lolled lifelessly out of the side of my mouth. I laid my head on the ground and instantly fell asleep. I was burned out, but I was happy and most important of all I was free.

I awoke with a start. It was still dark but I was aware that I was not alone. Slowly I flexed my aching muscles and struggled to sit up. The bush in front rustled and a rat ran across in front of me. I remember thinking that it was a shame he had run so quickly, he would have made a tasty snack, mind you I didn't have the energy to catch him, but it did remind me that I was hungry.

Shortly afterwards I saw a doglike creature, with a big bushy tail, dashing across the brush. It must have caught my scent because it veered round and made a beeline straight for me, stopping about ten metres away. We stared at each other; his eyes were light brown in colour and reflected the moon in a bright spangle at the corner. His back was sort of mid brown although his underbelly was much lighter, it looked almost white in the moonlight, his head looked as if he had been dipped in a pot of paint. The top half was a rusty brown colour but the bottom half was almost pure white; he had a sharp pointed snout with a small shiny black button nose on the end of it.

His ears stood erect similar to mine but they were shorter and a bit stubby and much furrier. He stood proud on slender, athletic legs of jet black, my attention was drawn again to that tail, I couldn't get over it, so lush and thick with a white flash at the end.

Slowly he moved toward me, his nose raised and twitching as he tasted the air and my scent. He must have concluded that I posed no threat to him because, seconds later, he turned gracefully and trotted away, with a bouncing gait, casting the occasional look over his shoulder just to check that I hadn't moved. I sat stock still; anyway, I didn't have the energy to move. When he had disappeared from view I lie down and once more drifted into an exhausted sleep.

The next time I woke the sun was already high in the sky. I felt partially refreshed but with uncharacteristic stiffness in my muscles. It took me a few moments to realise where I was, I half expected that it had all been a mad dream and that I was back in the shed with the other dogs. It hadn't been a dream, this was cold reality.

Nervously I lifted my head and pushed my snout out from under the bush that had sheltered me through the night. I couldn't see any humans, or any other animals for that matter, so I plucked up the courage to stand and survey the scene. My camouflage bush was half way down a hillside, which continued to roll away beneath me. It was the same rough, brush covered, countryside that I had become accustomed to on the hunting trips. Further down the hillside there was an olive grove with all the trees in regimented rows.

This was my first day of freedom, I must confess to feeling rather isolated, I was on my own, nobody to help me but nobody to tell me what to do, it was a bit daunting. I felt excited and energised but also just a little bit frightened realising that I was young and very naive. Emerging completely from the bush more features became visible to me. There were a number of farmhouses, similar to the one I had been living in for the past five months, speckled across the hillside opposite and between was a valley with a dry rocky riverbed meandering along it. Behind me the hillside seemed to rise up to the sky. I decided I had to be brave if I was to survive on my own so I clambered up the rise to see what was on the other side. The top of the hill proved to be quite a good vantage point. The terrain now fell away from me on all sides and was that familiar mix of rough brush, rocky nothingness and concentrated areas of olive and almond trees for as far as I could see.

Again I saw white farmhouses sprinkled all over the landscape, with a network of rough dusty dirt tracks curling round the undulations in the hillsides seemingly connecting them all to one another. Behind these hills there soared a great big mountain which had the same kind of terrain on its lower slopes but the higher up I looked the more the terrain became stark and rocky, completely lacking in vegetation. The mountain was the biggest thing I had ever seen and it dwarfed everything else.

There was another valley directly in front of me, similar to the one on the other side of the hill, but this one had a clutch of houses nestled together in the bottom with the obligatory small dry stream winding between them. There appeared to be no humans about but I could hear the faint barking of dogs. They were not saying anything of interest, just local chatter.

My stomach grumbled reminding me once more that I was hungry, in fact I was very hungry. I realised that I had not eaten since the night before my escape and all that running had used up my reserves of strength, I needed food and most of all water. I felt sure there must be food in the cluster of houses at the bottom of the valley, but there was also a greater risk of humans being about, so I decided to have a look around the farms first to see what I could scavenge.

I moved nervously around the hillside, constantly looking around me for any unusual movement and carefully circled around the village and up the other side of the valley toward the first farmhouse. I kept close to a white stone wall that encircled the property, I jumped onto the wall, the yard looked deserted, I slipped off the wall into the yard. Cautiously I moved toward the house. It looked surprisingly similar to the one I had been brought up in, so much so that I had to do a quick double take just to make sure fate hadn't dealt me a cruel blow and sent me back there.

All seemed quiet so I crept across the yard. Suddenly I had the fright of my life. The largest, and most ferocious, dog I have ever seen leapt from behind a pile of firewood, and charged toward me. He stopped abruptly when he was about ten metres from me, dipped his head, and growled a warning from somewhere deep within his gut. His bloodshot eyes inspected me, obviously weighing up the level of threat that I posed. Drool escaped from the length of his mouth and dripped messily onto the earth at his feet, the growl deepened becoming menacing. I was transfixed with terror, I had to do something. Fight or flight? Well fight was definitely out of the question.

"It's alright," I whimpered nervously, "I only want a little bit of food, if you have some to spare that is, I'm starving." He licked his lips, slobber dripping once more onto the dirt; he tilted his head slightly to one side as if thinking what to do. I took a huge risk and crept forward about a metre. That seemed to act as a trigger to him, he bared his teeth and charged toward me, the growl transforming into a thick hoarse snarl.

"I'm gonna tear your bum off." He spat the words at me. I wasn't going to wait around to see whether he would or not, I didn't want to risk losing my bottom, I turned tail and ran as fast as my tired legs would carry me. He was so much bigger and stronger than me, and obviously so much better fed, that he gained on me quickly. I was terrified; I knew it would only be a matter of seconds before I would feel a set of teeth in my rear end. Suddenly I understood what it was like to be a rabbit with me, or one of my buddies, on its tail.

He was only half a length behind me, I was frantically trying to pull my rear physically nearer to my head preserving my precious tail, when I heard the most awful clanking, crunching noise followed by a deep gurgling sound. Full of fear I ventured a glance over my shoulder and saw him lying on his back with his legs in the air.

At first I couldn't understand what had happened to him until, quickly regaining his feet, he strained against a thick steel chain that had brought his chase to such an abrupt end. I had not realised that he was chained to the wall, but luckily for me I had just managed to escape his sphere of operation and had been saved by the length of his tether. I stopped and gave him a victorious look, the bravery of success getting the better of me, I poked my nose in the air and sauntered nonchalantly away. His guttural snarl continued until I was out of sight. I felt good inside but even more tired and a whole lot hungrier. Something had to be done.

I selected another farmhouse and tried again. Cautiously I approached keeping a wary eye out for another guard dog, there didn't seem to be one. I peered through a gap in the boundary wall and quickly took in the scene. There was a rough dirt yard and a small covered terrace with a table and benches, similar in many ways to the one back by the shed.

On the table I spied a white plastic bag. I sampled the air, the bag was giving off a pleasant foody type aroma. I looked all around again in case I had missed something. Still no guard dog or human appeared so slowly I slunk through the gap and into the yard. Walking in a crouched position I approached the table. Still all clear. Silently I clambered onto the table top and gingerly sniffed at the bag, sure enough there was the aroma of dry stale meat, my mouth would have watered had I not have been so thirsty. I put my paw on the bag, gripped the side with my teeth and pulled. The plastic gave easily and the contents exploded onto the table, bits of food, tin cans, cartons and a wine bottle went in all directions. The cans and the bottle rolled noisily across the table before crashing onto the terracotta tiles below making a terrific noise. The bottle smashed into a thousand shards and the cans clattered toward the door of the house. I froze. I heard the sound of rapid movement coming from within as I stared at the doorway, transfixed, a large female human swept out and onto the terrace brandishing a broom.

"Get outa here!" Came the angry shout as the broom swept an arc through the air and came to rest with a thwack on my rear end. I made a quick grab at a shred of meat that poked from beneath a cardboard box, turned and made a swift exit. The overweight human lumbered across the yard after me. Hampered by her excess weight she stopped by the wall and stooped to grab a large stone from the ground. She pitched it after me, missing by only centimetres. She was putting her weight to good effect.

"Take that you mangy mongrel." She shouted as she pitched a second rock after me. Unfortunately for me, her aim was better than her running and the rock caught me just below my left ear. It hurt. I ran back up the hillside, all the time keeping a firm grip on the sliver of rotting meat, until I was wrapped in the safety of my bush again. I slumped on the ground, once more exhausted, and quickly devoured the scrap of meat.

It tasted good but was so minute that all it succeeded in doing was stimulating my appetite making me feel hungrier than ever. This course of events could not be allowed to continue, my food gathering escapade had proved to be a total disaster, I was still famished and my mouth was as dry as the dusty hillside. If nothing else I had proved to myself that I wasn't very adept at this scrounging, foraging game and I realised that unless I did something drastic, and soon, I could easily starve to death.

Then it came to me like a bolt out of the blue, why hadn't I thought of it before? I suppose my tiredness must have slowed my mind. Why not do what I do best, what my instincts should have told me to do. There was plenty of food all around me just waiting to be caught. I stirred myself, lowered my snout to the ground and took off at a tired, loping trot searching for the unmistakable scent of a delicious rabbit.

I quartered the hillside without success and decided to move my search into the olive grove further down the hillside, the trees would afford the rabbits more cover so it was a natural location for them to congregate. If there were rabbits around here I would be sure to find them. With my nose almost touching the ground I threaded through the trees until a scent brought me up short. Got it. No doubt about it, it was rabbit and it was fairly fresh. I followed the trail, it led me eventually to a hole in the ground, unmistakably the entrance to their warren. I pushed my snout as far into the hole as I could and tasted the air, the scent was fresh, this was an active warren.

Obviously with my size I couldn't go down the burrow after the rabbits, not that I would have fancied doing it if I had been small enough, so I would have to wait for them to come to me. I positioned myself a few metres from the entrance and waited; and waited.

The sun began its afternoon slide down the sky, the day began to cool. I was relieved to have had the shade of the trees during the hottest part of the day but even so it had been a hot and dry wait. My hunger was painful now, I was famished and parched, for I had tasted neither food nor water for almost forty eight hours, apart from the morsel that I stole from the rubbish bag, that is.

Daylight faded and the evening brought a gathering darkness to the world; still I waited. I began to wonder, had my nose deceived me? Were there rabbits here after all or had they detected me and used another exit? I decided to give it until moonrise and if there was no sign of rabbit by then I would be forced to move on.

I lie motionless, my mind beginning to wander, my stomach rumbling like a gathering thunderstorm. It was so loud I thought any rabbit in that hole would have been sure to have heard it. I was just contemplating giving up the hunt when my nose detected an almost imperceptible strengthening of the scent. It was only the powerful sensors deep inside my skull that could detect it, but it was there none the less. I stared at the hole, willing my dinner to emerge. There it was, a twitching snout, testing the air, I was grateful that I had taken the precaution of lying downwind so that they would not catch my scent.

Patiently I continued my wait, immobile amongst the dry brown grass, my mouth itching with anticipation. Slowly not one, not two but three rabbits emerged and hopped off to some nearby tufts of green shoots. That was it, I could wait no longer, my stomach overruled my head and I sprang up and made after the biggest of the three. He was late in seeing me, obviously overconfident in his cover, even so he was still able to establish a metre start. We careened off down the slope, both straining every sinew, both desperate for survival. This was the thrill of the hunt, already I could taste his sweet meat in my mouth. He jinked right, I veered, he jinked left, I veered, there was now a bigger gap between us! What's going on? That's not how it should be. We tore between the trees, him jinking at every opportunity and putting more space between us. These weren't the rules, I should be gaining on him.

With all the running, jinking and constant direction changes I had lost my sense of where we were and I hadn't realised which way we were headed, so it came as a complete surprise to me when we arrived back at the burrow and he dived headlong for safety, disappearing in a flash of white tail. My dinner had escaped me. I couldn't believe it, what a crucial time to fail.

Sadly, with my head down, I traipsed back the way I had come, it was foolish to expect them to reappear for a couple of hours or more, they knew I was there, they would be extra cautious next time. I headed once more for the security of the bush which seemed to have become my new home. Despondently I slumped beneath the bush and slept another uncomfortable, famished night.

I awoke just as dawn was beginning to cast a faint brightness across the eastern sky. I opened my weary eyes, lifted my head slightly and was rewarded with a wonderful sight. There before me was a family of rabbits, six of them, all busily feeding just a few metres from my bush. This time I decided that success was more important than size, so I fixed my attention on the youngest and smallest of the family, hopefully being a juvenile he would not be as crafty as last night's quarry. I crouched, ready for the chase to begin, my haunches twitching slightly from left to right in preparation for the initial lunge. I was conscious of the fact that I had not done any muscle stretches that morning and that I was risking a pulled muscle but I had to take the chance. Pulling a muscle now would prevent me from chasing a rabbit for a few days so it was a huge risk that I was taking but I was also aware that should I do any stretching the movement would frighten the nervous family off.

I made ready. I sprang toward the group and scattered them in six different directions, which neither surprised nor bothered me because I had concentrated all of my attention and skills on one rabbit in particular. This time although he jinked from right to left I found that I was gaining on him. He tried to circle round, I guessed toward their burrow, but I was having none of it I drove him downhill away from safety. Running downhill I was more surefooted than him, because of my long legs. When he had to leap over a small rock he lost his footing momentarily, landed heavily and stumbled, that was my chance, I was on him in no time at all.

I held him with my front paws as I clamped my jaws firmly round his juvenile, bony chest, and crushed the life out of him.

Ecstatically I carried the limp form back to my bush and settled down to enjoy my first food in over sixty hours. I wasted nothing as fur, bones, ears and feet filled my empty stomach. The entrails were especially delicious because the gore partially assuaged my thirst too. I know that sounds a bit barbaric in the cold light of day but you have to realise that his meat was the only way I could get food and avoid starving to death while his gore gave me moisture to prevent myself dying of thirst. It was a simple case of him or me, today it was me, I was the victor.

Feeling comfortable again for the first time in ages I lie down under the bush and waited out the hottest part of the day.

Over the next few days I experienced limited success with the rabbits. I chased many of them but the large ones seemed to be able to escape me all too easily whereas the younger, small ones that I did manage to catch provided scant nourishment. They did keep me alive, but only just. I did manage to catch the odd rat or vole but they presented no more than a mouthful, a different flavoured snack. My biggest concern as ever, was water. I only managed to find little bits here and there and had become reduced to licking the dew off the bush in the early morning to subsidise the meagre fluid I was getting from the small rabbits and rodents.

I could tell that I was losing weight and I felt so tired all the time, then there were these horrible little black things that I kept finding on my skin. They itched interminably, especially when I tried to nibble them off with my little front teeth. I had noticed that every so often one of them would drop off of its own accord but it always seemed to be replaced by two or three new ones.

I discovered that I was not alone on the hillside either. Twice I had seen the other doglike creature, one time he was accompanied by another adult and a pup. One day I spotted a human walking the hillside with two shaggy dogs and about a hundred strange creatures, the likes of which I had never seen before. These creatures were of a similar size to a large dog but were very thin with angular faces and large ears that stuck out sideways. They were very bony and their spindly legs seemed far too delicate to hold their weight. On their rump was a short fluffy tail that constantly flicked at the cloud of flies that followed their every move. Although they showed no fear they watched me constantly out of the corner of very peculiar eyes, they were like an orb of light green with a black slit, not the pupil that all other animals I had encountered seemed to have. Worst of all, for them, they had a big bag that swung uncomfortably between their rear legs. I knew that they posed no threat to me because all they seemed to do the whole day was eat and pass wind. Every now and then they would pause in their attempt to strip the vegetation and chew a mouthful of food in a very strange way; their jaws seemed to go sideways, not up and down like mine, almost as if they were grinding their food and not chewing it. I kept my distance, not because of any fear of these creatures but because of the human who accompanied them, after all every time I had come into contact with a human so far it had resulted in some sort of pain for me.

After about a week I decided that it was high time I moved on to new hunting grounds where I could, hopefully, find more abundant, and I hoped slower, rabbits to catch and also be closer to an important supply of water. With some reluctance I left the sanctuary of my bush for the last time as dawn broke and trotted away with hope in my heart and a young rabbit in my stomach.

I roamed for a couple of days, occasionally finding the odd morsel to eat, until, one afternoon I stumbled upon a group of houses. There were more houses here than I had ever seen in one place before, I guessed that this was what the humans referred to as a village. There was a hard black track, which I later found out is called a road, running between the houses and at the side of this road were two big wheelie bins that gave off a very inviting smell. I looked around, there was nobody in sight so I trotted smartly over the road and hopped up onto the top of the first bin, at least I thought I was hopping onto the top, but there was no top, so I tumbled headfirst into the bin. I landed in a heap, literally, a heap of rubbish and that was when I realised that these were in fact rubbish bins. I struggled to stand on the top of the stinking detritus to find myself covered in old tissues, plastic bags, cartons and old tin cans. My first instinct was to jump straight out again, but I stopped myself just in time. There was a pleasant aroma coming from the plastic bag under my forepaws. I bent down and ripped it open and to my utter delight discovered some scraps of meat and a couple of juicy chop bones that were liberally covered in fatty meat. There was some mouldy cheese and a lump of bread. Now that might not sound like delicious fare to you but believe me to a starving dog this was like manna from heaven.

Eagerly I devoured it, followed by some sauce from one of the old cans, I think it had contained baked beans because it tasted like tomato sauce. I found another tin that originally had some tuna fish in it and I licked the olive oil from the sides with gusto, until I cut my tongue. My stomach felt almost full for the first time since running away from my human.

Suddenly I froze. I could hear a rather familiar and frightening roaring sound, but I couldn't quite place it. I was curious to find out why that noise should make me feel scared. My inquisitiveness got the better of me and proved to be almost disastrous, I stood on my hind legs and peered over the rim of the bin, I couldn't believe my eyes. The roaring noise belonged to a car which was disappearing down the road. It was not just any car, it was a four by four with a small box trailer attached to the back and amazingly I recognised it as the one belonging to my human, a shudder ran down my spine. I could clearly see Big Blackie in the back and guessed that the others were hidden within the shadows.

I scrabbled out of the bin as fast as I could, driven by fear, I would explore the second bin some other day, for now I thought it a good idea to put as much distance between me and that particular human as was possible. I was running down the road in the opposite direction when I was brought up short by a faint tinkling sound, I inclined my head and turned it slowly until my radar ears located the direction from which the sound came. I could hardly believe my ears. All thoughts that the cruel human was nearby went completely out of my head as I ran toward the noise. Rounding a corner, I spied the source of the delightful sound, it was like the music of angels playing in my ears. Before me stood a large stone trough, with a metal spout sticking out of the rough stonework above it that spewed forth fresh clear water. The trough was filled to the brim and excess water trickled from one end to meander down the edge of the road and disappear into a drain. I was so thirsty that I lost control. Abandoning any semblance of caution and with the human and his four by four just a distant memory, I ran and sprang, full length, into the cool refreshing water, making a big splash which soaked the ground for a couple of metres around. Eagerly I slobbered up as much water as I could, it tasted so sweet, better than any water I had ever tasted before in my life. I drank until I felt bloated.

My tank full I stood for a while and let the coolness soothe my hot tired paws before dragging myself reluctantly out of the refreshing tub. I shook myself violently, my ears slapping against the top of my head and a huge arc of cool water showering like a garden sprinkler. I trotted off, gleefully, in search of somewhere nearby that I could make my home, somewhere to hide away from humans but still be within striking distance of this sleepy village. With this abundance of food and water I could see no reason for me to roam any further. Then I thought of a reason, that evil hunter, maybe all humans were evil, it would be prudent to avoid all contact with humans in future.

I discovered an area of dry shrubbery about three hundred metres outside the village and within it I located a large bush that would provide me with adequate cover. Wrapped within its safe cloak I would be invisible to any passing human and I prepared to make it my new home. The food and drink had made me feel like an over inflated balloon and very lethargic so I circled round a few times to flatten the ground and lie down to sleep, comfortable at last. I belched. All the indications were that this would be an idyllic place to live, plenty of food, all the water I could drink and a soft warm bed too; it was heavenly.

    I rose late the following morning, stretched and considered what I would like to do in my new found paradise. Breakfast, I thought, that would make a good start, maybe it would be a good idea to go and explore the second rubbish bin to see what delicacies it held, maybe I would find some more delicious meat. Happily I trotted to the bins and leapt into the one that I didn't get to explore the day before. I hit the floor with a painful thud; it was empty. That came as a bit of a shock but, undaunted, I picked myself up and crouched ready to spring into the original bin. It was an easy leap but as I was flying between the bins I made a heartbreaking discovery. The bins had been emptied overnight, the original bin was empty too. I couldn't stop in mid air so I crashed painfully into the plastic emptiness. Both bins were devoid of any food, I would have no breakfast today.

Feeling somewhat disappointed I struggled out from the bin and landed lightly on the warm tarmac within a metre of two young boys who had, unbeknown to me, been walking to the bins to dump some rubbish. I don't know who was the most surprised, me or them. We stared at each other for a moment, motionless, unsure of what each other would do. It didn't take long for me to find out. They dropped the plastic bags they had been carrying and one of the boys lashed a kick in my direction, catching me in the ribs. As he did so his accomplice scraped up a handful of stones which he proceeded to hurl in my direction, some catching me on my head and others on my side, fortunately my coat seemed to prevent me from sustaining any bruising. The remainder of the stones clattered off the bins and the tarmac as the boys began shouting at me, trying to chase me away. That's all it took, I turned tail and ran, not because of their shouting, that had no effect on me, but I had noticed that they were scooping up more handfuls of stones which they proceeded to launch after me. Luckily for me the accuracy of their aim was no match for the female human, when I invaded her farm a few days earlier, and the shower of stones rattled off the bins and bounced up the road. I sprinted away from them and headed for the sanctuary of the brush.

Lying within the safety of my bush I licked my wounds, some of the stones had cut my underbelly after all, although there was nothing serious. I felt despondent, the place I had hoped would provide me with a comfortable home had turned a bit sour, maybe it would be an unfortunate one off. I resolved that, a few hours later, when I expected the boys would have gone home, I would wander back into the village and perhaps by then somebody would have thrown some scraps of food into the vacant bins. Most of all, being thirsty, a visit to the trough would be mighty welcome.

In the late afternoon I wandered down the road toward the water trough and noticed there was a human there filling a plastic water bottle. I ventured a little nearer, prepared to wait until he had completed filling the bottle before moving in for my drink. No such luck, when he saw me approaching he began shouting and waving his arms around in an effort to frighten me. I thought it a bit pathetic in all honesty, he didn't frighten me at all, I continued to approach the trough. With that he bent down and shovelled up a handful of stones which he proceeded to propel in my direction.

One or two caught me but they only bounced off my fur without causing any noticeable pain. Once again I headed for the safety of my bush, I would have to be extremely careful when I went to the village from now on.

It didn't seem such a perfect place to make my home any more.

For the next few days I visited the village at different times, experimenting, trying to identify the safest time of day, but there always seemed to be humans about, all very keen to throw stones at me. I had to be very careful when I scavenged the bins too, one time I was happily pulling a few scraps of food out of a plastic bag, oblivious to what was going on around me, when a human peered over the side of the bin wielding a stick. He managed to get in a couple of painful blows before I could get away. Another valuable, if painful, lesson I had learned, constant vigilance, it seems one can never be completely safe with humans around, best be continuously on your guard. I fared no better at the water trough either, there always seemed to be a human close enough to discourage me from getting a drink, usually armed with a walking stick or a handful of stones.

I cast my mind back and pondered on the first day that I had ventured into the village, it had been a unique day when everybody must have been asleep or something because I never found it deserted ever again.

I have to be honest and say that all this aggression from the villagers was not solely aimed at me. There were one or two other dogs that roamed the streets of the village searching and competing for the meagre scraps of food. They were all very friendly toward me, I suppose because we were all in the same situation, we were all starving, literally, our ribs were clearly visible beneath our ever tightening skin as we searched constantly for something to fill the aching void within our gut. Any scraps, no matter how small, were viciously fought over. Even something as common as water was a problem. The village trough was perpetually overflowing, running to waste, but we were animals and the population saw it as some sort of violation for us to dare to drink it. We were, as often as not, denied the opportunity to lap up that basic commodity and as a result were all pretty thirsty most of the time. The others, who had been around the village far longer than me, had scratches that had turned to sores and cuts that seeped, attracting flies that fed on the foetid septic fluid. All in all they were a pathetic pack, was that my destiny too? No way, I decided, I had more about me than that, I was too intelligent to roll over and accept this as my fate.

We all came in for the same treatment from the humans of the village, we were constantly pelted with stones and chased away almost as if it was just a game. Perhaps it was an amusing game to them but for us it was serious, it was a game of life or death. It seemed more and more to me as if the first day I had arrived there had been a fluke. This village had no compassion.

I don't want to appear to be unkind to my fellow canines but the other dogs didn't really have much of a brain between them, they were quite happy to be abused every day for the chance of a few scraps of food. This was not enough for me, I was convinced that there was something better for me out there, and I was determined to seek it out.

So it happened that after a couple of weeks in the village I bade a fond farewell to my new acquaintances and took to the open mountainsides in search of my destiny, but I made sure I had a few scraps, and a long drink from the gutter, before I left. The pack, to a dog, thought I was mad to go, I was off my trolley and could never survive on the barren mountain alone. They thought I would stand a better chance within their pack, but I knew better.

I roamed for a couple of weeks, I found one or two locations that were promising but still I wanted more, I always had a feeling in my gut that there was something better for me, just over the next hill.

Eventually I arrived on the top of a hill that overlooked the Mediterranean Sea to the south and a small village to the north. There were five houses built beside a rough dirt track that ran along the top of the ridge. I could see no humans but, despite that, the place had a friendly feel to it. More than that there was a good supply of rabbits. They had a network of burrows, I discovered, under the terrace of one of the houses and under the swimming pool of two of the others. The way the houses looked, and the fact that four of them had swimming pools told me that these were not the kind of humans I had become used to, they were definitely not farmers.

It didn't take me long to catch a rabbit for my dinner and I settled down under a cactus bush, growing conveniently close beside the dirt track, to eat it. I concealed myself as best I could by lying close to a wire fence that ran behind the clump of cactus. I was happily crunching my way through a tasty bit of hip.

"Hello then!"

Where did that come from? I looked all around and saw nothing.

"Over here." My ears followed the sound and there, behind the wire fence, lying there scratching himself, was a medium sized, friendly looking dog. He had a dark shaggy coat, soft brown eyes and a laid back air. I stopped eating.

"What's your name then?"

"Erm! Well they call me Girl."

"Girl is it? I don't know but these humans are really inventive aren't they, I'm called Boy." I didn't tell him that my human hadn't given me a name at all and that Girl was what Earhole had called me.

"Where you from then?" Enquired the shaggy fellow. I was a bit non-plussed, I was hungry and wanted to eat without being disturbed, also I had never been spoken to in this casual, carefree way before.

"Erm! Here and there you know."

"Erm, Here and there? Where's that then?"

"Over the hills, a long way over in that direction." I nodded my head in any general direction, I honestly had no idea exactly where I had come from.

"Over the hills a long way! So what brings you all the way over here then?"

"Well actually I'm trying to eat my dinner." I said testily.

"Ooooh sorree." He stretched the end of the word sarcastically. Instantly I felt remorse at my remark.

"No, I'm sorry, that was rude of me." I apologised, feeling guilty for the way I had spoken to him, especially as he seemed such a friendly chap. He didn't seem to mind though, he just scratched behind his ear and then under his chin. "Actually, I have run away from my human."

"Run away have you? Why's that then?"

"Because my human is a cruel person, he used to beat me and the other dogs with a big stick, and he did something with my mother, and he killed Dozy." It all came gushing out in a garbled muddle of words.

"Steady on gal, one bit at a time. Who's these other dogs then? Where are they all then?"

I told him about mother disappearing, about the beatings the human meted out to us if we didn't do what he wanted us to, the hunting expeditions and what had happened to Dozy. He listened intently, every now and then inclining his head first to one side then the other, as if having difficulty concentrating. Every so often he asked me a question, which inevitably ended with the word 'then'. When I had finished he looked at me with a sad expression and tutted.

"So, you gonna stay here then?"

"I don't know yet, what's it like here anyway?"

"Oh it's alright, everybody seems to be friendly, especially the bloke who's coming along now." I looked about but I couldn't see anybody.

"Who? There isn't anybody about."

"You just wait gal, regular as clockwork he is, set your clock by him. About nuther fifteen seconds."

We waited and sure enough over the brow of the hill came this bronzed human. He was not that tall and very slim, in fact he looked reminiscent of Gandhi, with a nice lived in looking face. I can't describe him any more accurately because my attention was immediately taken by the most beautiful dog I have ever seen, walking sedately beside him. He was similar to a German Shepherd in colouring and build but slightly smaller and much more handsome, with the most stunning eyes. They were edged in black, making it look as if he were using eyeliner, they looked similar to the eyes of an Egyptian pharaoh. They were crowned with the most gorgeous eyelashes I had ever laid eyes on. I swooned; it was definitely love at first sight. The dog was on the end of a rope but walked beside his human quite happily, every now and then looking up at him with obvious affection in his eyes. He could look at me that way any time he wanted, I thought.

I watched as they approached, the human saw me and made a move toward me. I cringed, expecting a blow from the big stick that I had only just noticed him carrying. I admit that I was frightened but I needn't have been, he fondled my ear for a short while before moving on.

"C'mon Samson." He said softly.

"So that's his name. Samson. What a beautiful name." My mind was in a cloud.

"Meanwhile back in the real world then!" Boy had a look of boredom on his face.

"Sorry. What did you say?" I wrenched my attention away from Samson for a millisecond.

"So! You stayin' then?"

"Um, maybe for a while, see how it goes, you know." My gaze followed Samson as he walked majestically beside his human.

"Yeah! You're stayin' then."

Yes I was staying, if only for another chance to see Samson. When I had finished my meal I had a long talk with Boy. He told me that his human was a kind man who looked after him well. He was working at the airport in Malaga, where they were building a large extension, so he was out for most of the day. Boy spent his days lazing around scratching himself as far as I could gather.

Of the other houses, he told me that two had owners who came and went several times a year, they had a second home somewhere else but Boy did not know where, and the last house had humans in permanently, they didn't have a dog and kept themselves to themselves, but Boy assured me that they were very friendly. I looked quizzically at the wire fence that completely encompassed the house and yard that Boy was in. It was about two metres high and I could not identify any gaps, save the double gates that opened onto the track, a strong chain and padlock held them firm.

"So, how do you get out of your yard?"

"Get out of my yard? Why would I want to do that then?"

"Well, so that you can chase rabbits, run about and have a bit of freedom."

"Chase rabbits? Run around? Sounds rather energetic that does. Why would I want to do that then?"

"To catch rabbits and things, you know food, and to have fun."

"Nah, I get all the food I need from my human and I can have plenty of fun without running around."

"Well, what about freedom, the ability to go wherever you want whenever you want."

"Sounds like hard work to me gal." A smug smile came across his face, he lifted his chin up and scratched his neck, the disc on his collar rattled. "Trust me gal freedom isn't all it's cracked up to be. My human gives me everything I need, what would I want with freedom then?"

"I don't think I could give up my freedom now, I've had to work too hard for it."

"We'll see then!"

Just then a car came over the hill and stopped by the gate in the fence. The driver got out, twisted a key in the padlock, slipped the chain and opened the gate. Returning to his car he drove into the yard, closing the gate behind him, all the time watching me closely. He strode into the house with Boy bounding excitedly after him, he was obviously Boy's human.

A few minutes passed and the door to the house opened again, Boy's human stepped out with a bowl in each hand and wandered over toward the gate. He placed both bowls on the floor close to me and smiled. One was full of food and the other was full of water.

"You look as if you could do with these. There you go Girl."

"How did he know my name then?" Oh my goodness he's got me saying it too now!

For the first time I realised that some humans could be good to know, they could be kind and thoughtful if they wanted to be. Samson's human had been gentle to me and Boy's human had been thoughtful, perhaps not all humans were cruel, but I still intended to be wary. I thought I might hang around for a couple of days and spend my time catching rabbits or talking to Boy or more probably both. I might even try and get to know Samson.

The next evening Boy's human came careening along the track as usual, swept into the drive in a cloud of dust, parked his car and disappeared into the house. A couple of minutes later he emerged with a bowl of food for Boy and another for me which he placed on the ground before topping up both our water bowls. I kept a curious eye on him as I ate my way to the bottom of the bowl. When he went to the rear of his car and opened the tailgate my interest level went up a notch. I was a bit concerned, would he try to lure me into the car I wondered? I didn't like the thought of being in a car again, it brought back memories of the hunter's four by four and the trailer.

To my surprise he lifted a large wooden packing crate out of the car and proceeded to put it beside the cactus bush that I had made my home. Returning to his car he produced some blankets and an old sleeping bag.

"Here you go Girl." He said softly. "I've got you a nice warm kennel and some blankets that the guys at work had going spare." He spread the blankets over the base of the crate, laid the sleeping bag on top and stepped back to admire his work. "That should keep you warm and dry now that the nights are getting a bit colder." He ruffled my ear and disappeared into the house.

"What's all that then?" Guess who?

"It's a sort of house I suppose. Your human said it will keep me warm and dry."

"Warm and dry eh! I've got some blankets of my own indoors."

I hadn't really noticed it before but the days and especially the nights had become somewhat cooler lately.

It was the end of October, and I was almost seven months old.

Every morning and evening, regular as clockwork, Samson and his human would walk over the brow of the hill and on past the other houses, after a hundred metres or so he would turn around and retrace his steps, disappearing over the hill from whence he came. The first day I lie there and looked up into Samson's beautiful eyes as he strutted proudly by. The second day I got to my feet and followed a few metres behind him. The third day I summoned up all my courage and walked proudly beside him.

"Do you pass by here often?" I asked shyly.

"Oh please! Is that the best you can come up with?" Samson was not impressed with my ice breaking line I could tell. "You know I do, I come by twice a day, morning and evening. You watch me do it for heaven's sake!" I hoped that I hadn't blown it. I dropped my head a bit.

"Come on, we can talk while we walk, my man John will never know."

So, it seemed that some humans had names too, Gandhi was really John. Samson was either an exceptionally kind dog or he had taken a shine to me, I fervently hoped that it was the latter. We absorbed ourselves in inconsequential chit chat and by the time the walk was at an end we had become really comfortable in each other's company.

"We are almost back at your home so I had better go to my crate." I was disappointed to have to leave his company but I didn't think John would want me around his house.

"Come home and lie on my terrace with me we can really get to know each other." I relished the invitation.

"What about John? Will he be alright with me coming home with you?"

"Don't worry about mum and dad, they won't mind, they are animal lovers and dad likes you I can tell." So I walked onto the terrace with Samson, fully expecting to be ushered off at any moment.

"I thought you said his name was John but you just called him dad."

"That's what we call humans who are special to us and take us into their home." He explained. "We call the female human mum and the man dad. It's a way of showing affection." I wondered if I would ever have a mum and dad.

We relaxed together in the shade of the terrace and Les, that was the name of Samson's mum, gave us both a hide chew to gnaw on. She also made a big fuss of me and made me welcome whenever I turned up at their home. I liked it there.

Samson asked how I came to be on the mountain so I told him my story, leaving nothing out. When I had finished he smiled at me.

"You are a very strong willed and brave girl aren't you."

"Oh I don't know about that, I just knew that I could never bear to be just a puppy factory. I wanted more out of life so I went for it."

"Yes, but think about it, all of the others in the hunter's pack hated to be there but not one even attempted to become free, they just accepted the cards fate dealt them."

"I suppose so."

"And the pack in the village, they accepted being stoned rather than look for a better life. Not you. You were prepared to risk everything to realise your dream, I admire you for that." Outwardly I gave him a sheepish, embarrassed look but inside I was thinking that he was right and I should be proud of myself.

"How about you Samson? How did you end up with your John and Les?"

"My story is nowhere near as interesting as yours, I haven't been brave or adventurous like you girl, I've just been incredibly lucky."

"I'd still like to hear it." He laid his chin on his extended front legs and began his story.

Apparently when he was just a few weeks old a fox attacked him and his family. When his mother saw the fox approaching she had pushed all the pups into a ditch in a desperate effort to protect them, but all his siblings had just lain there exposed in the bottom of the ditch while Samson had crawled under some rubbish and lie perfectly still and silent. Sadly his mother died protecting her puppies, and his brothers and sisters had been discovered and killed too. Lying motionless under the rubbish had shielded him from the fox and as a consequence he was the only one to survive.

When morning came he crawled out from the rubbish and cowered by himself in the undergrowth.

During the afternoon there was a tremendous storm and as the rainwater gushed through the ditch he was almost swept away. Fortunately for him that was when John and Les drove past and completely by chance Les noticed him floundering in the deluge. They stopped and rescued him, cold, hungry, soaked through and alone and had taken him home with them. The rest, as they say was history, he stayed with them and they became his mum and dad, he was very happy, well looked after and loved enormously.

November brought a real change in the weather as winter began to settle in. The skies were darkened by a layer of deep grey, moisture laden cloud, the air felt heavy and muggy. Then came the rain, heavy at times, torrential at others, and continuing unabated for over a week. I was really grateful for my crate which Boy's dad had placed strategically so that the solid back faced into the prevailing wind ensuring that no rain penetrated my refuge. By curling up at the very back I was able to keep dry and relatively warm. The rain hammering down on my hollow wooden shelter gave it the property of a big base drum and I could only sleep when the hammering eased to a steady downpour.

That's how I spent the whole of the wet season, watching the rain sheet down from comparative safety, sleeping when possible and catching the odd rabbit when the rain let up sufficiently. In between downpours Samson would take a walk and I joined him eagerly for a talk, if not, on the rare days that he was outside, I would chat to Boy.

I didn't feel as fit or energetic as I had when I was a puppy because, despite the human's kindness, and unbeknown to me, I didn't really get sufficient nutrition and I became seriously underweight. I didn't know that a diet consisting solely of rabbit was insufficient to sustain life, it seems that you need to include different food, thank goodness for Boy's dad, he possibly saved my life. In addition to my lethargy I was still being plagued by these cursed black things which clung to me everywhere, I even had one on my eyelid.

Life settled down into a bit of a routine through those winter months until by mid February the weather began to warm significantly and I spent a bit more time roaming the mountain, still lethargic and hungry but happy in my world of freedom.

March came and unexpectedly my world came crashing down. It all began in a flurry of excitement one morning when Boy charged out of the house and bounded over to the fence to talk to me.

"Guess who's going home then?" He was obviously thrilled because he spun around as if chasing his tail.

"Going home? What do you mean going home?" My initial thought was that his dad, I still didn't know his name, had managed to find out where I had run away from and was going to return me to that hated hunter. I was terrified. Would I be forced to go on the run all over again?

"We're goin' home." Boy was so excited, his tail was wagging so hard I thought it might fly off, I soon realised his exuberance had nothing to do with my origins.

"Dad's contract is up and we are goin' back to our home in Madrid. Great innit?"

"Yes." I replied somewhat cautiously. "But where is this Madrid and what if I don't like it there?"

His tail stopped wagging immediately, he became rooted to the spot. His chin dropped and he stared at me with those soft brown eyes. There was a silence that you could have cut with a knife.

"I'm sorry Girl, but I don't think he's taking you with us."

"Oh!" My heart sank. I just stood there in disbelief, I wasn't wanted. I turned and sadly crawled to the rear of my crate and curled up. I had enjoyed five months of being spoiled but now it looked as if I would be abandoned, alone, to fend for myself all over again. I didn't want to be alone. I thought I was part of Boy's family. I knew that I couldn't live with Samson, even though John and Les were always especially kind to me and I was always welcome at his home, they had always made it clear that I could never be a part of the family. For the first time in a long while I cried myself to sleep that night.

Two days later and Boy's human stuck his head into my crate, he gave me some stale bread, filled my water bowl and tried to ruffle my ear but I shrank back so that he couldn't reach me. He had let me down and I didn't like him anymore. Boy was getting a comfortable new home, I was getting a few stale crusts.

"Bye then Girl, hope everything goes well for you." He turned and was gone. As the car swerved out of the drive, with the usual cloud of dust, I noticed Boy sitting upright by the tailgate looking out the rear window at me. He looked sad to be leaving, his head tilted the way it did whenever he was concentrating on listening to me talk to him. I saw him mouth the word 'goodbye' and I swear that I saw a tear in his eye, or was that the tear in mine? The car disappeared over the crest of the hill, and my friend was gone forever. It all happened so quickly that I didn't even get the chance to say a proper goodbye to him. I stared at the empty track and watched as the dust began to settle.

"Yes, bye then, don't worry about me, I'm a survivor I'll make it on my own." I honestly think that was the only time that I have felt let down, I was hurting inside. I cried. I cried because I had lost a close friend, I cried because I was alone again. I also believe that I cried because my health was slowly deteriorating. I had escaped from the hunter because I didn't like the violence, being hit and kicked, and I certainly didn't want to become a breeding machine. I hadn't escaped because I wanted to be alone and being with Boy and Samson for five months had convinced me that I certainly didn't want to be alone.

I wanted a permanent companion and after being spoiled, by my standards anyway, I had thought that there might be a kind human out there who would love me. I could give them so much love in return. John and Les loved me but there was no way that they were going to give me a permanent home. I still had Samson, he was a true friend, but I was depressed and feeling very sorry for myself.

I hid myself away for two whole days, I didn't even come out to walk with Samson. I heard him call me as he walked past but I ignored him. I regret that so much now because my petulance must have hurt him, but he never let it show and he never held it against me. Eventually, as ever, hunger got the better of me and I realised it was about time I snapped out of my self pity, so I had a scout around to see what food I could find. I suppose it would be back to a raw rabbit diet again.

It was dusk and I was wandering along the track, returning to my shelter when I noticed that there was a car in the driveway of the end house. That meant there must be humans too? If so, what were they like? I decided I would give them a wide berth for the moment. Boy had said that everybody who lived on the top of the mountain was kind but if that meant feeding me for a while and then abandoning me, well I could do without that sort of kindness. I felt sad for myself, these black things irritated to hell and it got worse if I scratched them, on top of that my snout was badly sunburnt, the skin peeling in lumps to leave painfully raw flesh underneath. I think I was suffering from what humans would call clinical depression.

Miserably I trudged along the track and was surprised to find that I recognised the car, I had seen it parked here a few times over the past five months. I knew that the people usually stayed for about three weeks and then they went away again for a while. Samson had said that they had something called 'work' in a foreign land and that was why they were not here all the time.

Passing close to the car I noticed that a female human was taking something out of the back. She turned and saw me. She stopped. I froze. She eyed me for a short while, her forehead creased and an expression of pity spread across her face.

"Hello sweetheart." Her voice was warm and kind sounding. "You look as if you could do with some food. Let's see what we can find for you." Where had I heard that before? Even so I lingered.

She disappeared down some steps and returned a few minutes later with an ice cream tub full of water and another with some sort of meat in it. Placing them both on the ground she stepped back, smiling, it was a different type of smile to all the ones I had seen previously, she didn't just smile with her mouth her whole face smiled. Instinct told me she was a kind human so slowly I moved toward the two tubs. I didn't take my eyes off her though, and as I began to eat I was ready to make a break for it if she made a wrong move. She approached me very slowly and ran her hands over my coarse matted hair. I moved on to the water and enjoyed the sweet tasting liquid, still keeping a wary eye on her, then back to the food.

When I had eaten my fill I moved away and went back to my crate not wishing to build my hopes up too high, only for them to be dashed later. I slept with a comfortable belly and a warm feeling that I could not explain. As I slept, for the first time in my life, I had a dream. I was inside the female human's house lying at her feet, on the cold tiled floor. The dream was so vivid but was this just a dream or was it a premonition?

The next day I felt very tired. It seemed to me these days that I was permanently tired. I could no longer catch mature rabbits, I located and roused them but as the chase progressed I discovered that I could not overhaul them, I could not get close enough for the kill, they always managed to escape as tiredness overcame my limbs. I had to settle for either the very small young ones, where my experience outweighed my speed, or the old ones where my speed still enabled me to catch them. Either way the meat was insufficient on the one hand and extremely tough on the other.

It was mid morning, I was lying despondently in my crate with my head resting on my front paws, staring out at my small square of world, lacking both the motivation and the strength to hunt, when I heard a car start. A couple of minutes later my new female human friend passed by, with a male human in the driving seat beside her, they were deep in conversation but it did not stop them peering into my meagre dwelling as they passed. I watched the car rumble over the crest of the hill and disappear. Alone again then, as Boy would have said.

It could have been no more than two hours later when the car emerged over the crest, followed by billows of dry dust, bounced down the track and swept into their drive. They must have been on a shopping expedition because they unloaded four big bags from the back of the car and carried them down the steps and out of sight. More in hope than expectation I meandered along the track in their general direction, I could always trot past if need be as if I were on one of my excursions. There was no need for pretence, as I came level with the flight of steps the female human emerged with a big bowl full of meat and gravy, just as I had hoped she would. I watched her climb the steps, my mouth began to water.

"Come here sweetheart," she called. It seemed as if my name had changed from Girl to Sweetheart, I wondered what sweetheart meant. She called to me again. Slowly I walked up to her as she placed the bowl on the ground. It smelled delicious. I fell on it eagerly, but I kept one eye on her.

Then an unusual thing happened, after I had eaten the food, she put her arms round my neck and cuddled me, I had never in my life had a cuddle before, I must admit I rather liked it. Instinctively I knew that this was a good human, I no longer felt any threat at all, I was instantly comfortable with her.

Yes I liked her but once more disappointment was to knock on my door, for the next few days I received food, very nourishing food, I received cuddles, lovely warm cuddles, but that was it. There was no move to give me anything other than food, water and hugs. That would have to be sufficient for now. Then on the fifth day, I think it was, I heard her talking to her male companion as I ate.

"Did you find out anything in the village? How long is Antonio away for?" Antonio? I guessed that was the name of Boy's dad.

"You won't believe this, but apparently his contract has been completed and he's gone back to Madrid for good."

"You've got to be joking!"

"No joke, she's been abandoned." It seems they thought that Boy and his dad had just gone away for a short holiday leaving me to fend for myself in the short term and that they were planning to return. Not so, and I could have told them if they had but asked me.

I could have told you that.

They didn't hear me.

I took the opportunity to dip my head a bit and look up at them sorrowfully so that the whites showed below my eyes. It usually worked with humans. They both knelt down and made a fuss of me, I received two cuddles no less. They were a warm and loving couple, I realised that I would like to stay with them. They could be to me what John and Les were to Samson. Some hope.

"Oh David, that's terrible, just to leave her like that." So he had a name too, just like John, this was David. I wondered what her name was.

"We will have to look after her for now Christine."

Ah so it's Christine, thank you David.

Pleased though I was to hear them talk of looking after me, the phrase 'for now' rankled a bit.

"I'll go and get her crate, see if she will stay in it on our drive."

"That sounds like a good idea."

Yes David that sounds like a really good idea.

He went up to my old home and carried my crate back, placing it in the sheltered corner beside his car. Was I moving in or was this only a temporary measure, I kept thinking of that phrase 'for now'. Again I had a few cuddles and my ears tickled for good measure. Christine ran her hands over my body, detecting the plump black visitors.

"You are so thin sweetheart, I think we need to feed you up a bit, don't you?" I liked the sound of that. Christine continued to stroke me gently.

"We need to do something about these tics too." David touched some of the black growths that had irritated me for so long. "Don't worry sweetheart, we'll look after you. We'll get you sorted."

I had a second bowl of food that night and, as the sun dipped in the sky, I crawled into my crate with mixed emotions playing games inside my head. There was one excited voice that realised I really liked Christine and David and I wanted to have the opportunity to stay with them permanently. There was, on the other hand, a worried voice that kept reminding me of the phrase 'for now' and told me that it would never happen. Confusion reigned.

I didn't want them to leave me or take me to somebody else. It was then that I remembered my dream, or premonition, maybe all it needed was a helping hand to become reality. I determined that I had better take things into my own hands and do something about it.

I had to come up with a strategy, I had a lot of thinking and planning to do.

I had to come up with a foolproof plan.

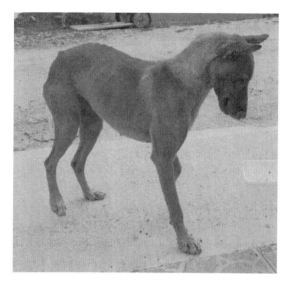

My first close encounter with Christine.

Thin and wasted, hungry and tic infested.

A loving touch of fuss from Christine.

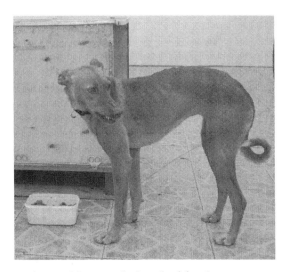

Very cautious with an early bowl of food.

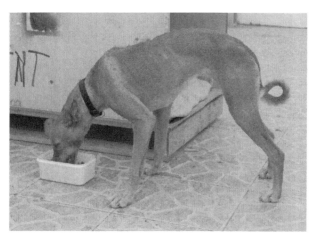

My crate moved to the drive and another big bowl of food.

My sunburnt and painful snout with soothing cream applied.

Enjoying a big hug and a brush from Christine.

Not enjoying being tied up for the first time.

Next morning I had another bowl of food for breakfast, but this time David and Christine stayed and watched to make sure that I finished it. I was suffering from malnutrition for heaven's sake, why wouldn't I eat it all.

When the bowl was licked clean David placed a leather collar around my neck, this pleased me because Samson had told me this was a mark of ownership. Was this also a statement of intent? David attached a short length of rope to the collar. Samson hadn't mentioned this. Gently he put one arm across my chest just below my neck, the other arm he placed around my rear end. He lifted me and placed me in the back of their car, it was a four by four, was this significant? I didn't know what was going on but for some inexplicable reason I had no fear, somehow I knew that everything would be alright.

They both climbed into the front of the car, David keyed the engine and off we drove, we were leaving the mountain. I refused to sit down, I wanted to know where we were going and what was happening. I had to lean as we went round the corners as if I were riding a motorcycle. Trying to keep my balance was tiring, I could still see out of the windows if I were sitting, so I sat. Still a bit tiring maybe I could still see out if I lie down. I lie down, in all honesty I was close to falling down and that would have damaged my pride.

The movement of the car made me feel strange inside. Compared to the hard bouncing I experienced in the trailer this journey was as if we were floating along. I began to feel queasy, I brought all my breakfast up in a big heap in the back of the car. I thought that I would be in deep trouble when it was discovered but no, when the car stopped I was gently lifted down to the pavement and fussed.

"Oh you poor sweetheart, you're not used to being in a car are you." Christine ruffled my ear and kissed me on the top of my head. "We can soon clear that up."

We walked along a busy pavement, I was bemused, I had never been in such a big village before, there were dozens of cars roaring around, not to mention a constant flow of humans on the pavement. Eventually Christine pushed through a glass door and we stepped into a cool room which had a lingering clinical smell. I could also detect the scent of other animals, many dogs, some cats and some that I could not identify as yet. Later I discovered that this was in fact a veterinary surgery and I was to get a full examination, whatever that was.

The vet had a name too, she was called Carolina, yes apparently all humans have names of their very own, she was brilliant and so gentle that I immediately felt at ease. She gave me a hug, she had never met me before and I got a hug, and she played with my ears for a while, followed by a quick inspection. She bent my ears back and looked into them carefully, this was followed by an examination of my teeth.

"I estimate that she is about twelve months old."

If you had asked me I could have told you that.

She felt my belly, squeezing me firmly but painlessly.

"She is not pregnant, which is good."

Too right I'm not.

Next I had a small pointed thing inserted into my bottom, this was uncomfortable but not painful. Finally she ran her hands gently over my whole body and touched a few of those horrible black things that I seemed to be able to grow with great ease. She made more fuss of me before turning to Christine and David and flashing a smile.

"She seems to be in good condition bearing in mind how she has been living, but she has a very high temperature which we must bring down. There are a few other things we need to attend to." I stood motionless, wondering what was coming next, the only movement I made was to turn my soft brown eyes upward sorrowfully showing the whites below. I tried to look as helpless as I could.

"The first thing we must do is get rid of these horrible tics, because they are sucking her blood and taking all the goodness out of her. That's why she is so painfully thin." Carolina explained, but she didn't stop there. "With this many she is very anaemic, if we do not treat them now it would not be long before she died."

I was stunned; I would die soon if they weren't removed. Oh my goodness!

Get them off me quickly, come on hurry, I'm too young to die.

So that was why I felt so tired all the time. I began to feel this might just be my lucky day.

While I stood still and silent Carolina went to a drawer and selected a syringe which she filled with medicine from a small bottle. She inserted the needle into my neck. It didn't hurt but almost immediately I experienced this strange burning sensation under my skin, it started where the needle had gone in and rapidly spread through my entire body. I don't know what was in that syringe but whatever it was these tic things obviously didn't like it because within a couple of minutes they began to drop off me. In no time at all there were masses littering the floor, making small red bloody blotches. They looked hideous, round bloated bodies apparently filled with my blood, comparatively big jaws and little legs that wriggled and kicked in their death throes.

When Carolina was satisfied that they had all released their grip on me her nurse swept the bloody mass into a dustpan and swabbed the floor with a mop.

"I think there were more than a hundred, which is a lot, no wonder she is so listless." Carolina gently stroked me again.

I remained standing with my tail curled firmly between my legs and my ears flat to my head, all this talk of illness and death had made me feel queasy. Mind you I was determined to take full advantage of the situation, all this sympathy must not be wasted. I knew that I desperately wanted to stay with Christine and David, and my gut feeling was that deep down they wanted to keep me so I made myself look as sad and helpless as I could. Time to drop my snout a bit and look up to show the whites of my eyes yet again.

Beside me Carolina filled another syringe.

More? What's this for?

"She probably has worms so we will give her a shot for that too." Carolina smiled. I didn't, the thought of me having worms wriggling around inside me made me feel sick again. I had to have a couple more injections to stop me getting an infection and to boost my appetite. I also had my first anti-rabies inoculation, I didn't know what that meant but what the heck, give me a shot of everything that's going, after all my neck was already beginning to resemble a pin cushion.

That wasn't the end of it either, I had some liquid put on my neck, all down my back and near my tail, this was apparently to get rid of fleas and other parasites and would stop the tics returning. My claws were trimmed and my coat brushed. Hey! I got the full beauty treatment.

By the time I arrived back at my crate I felt like a new girl, very tired but a whole lot more comfortable. I demolished another bowl of food and, although it was only early afternoon, I crawled into my crate and fell into a restful sleep.

I hadn't realised quite how bad my condition had become, how much I had deteriorated over the last six months. All that I was aware of was that I lacked energy. The tics had been sucking the life out of me, I was skin and bone thanks to them and a poor diet, my coat was extremely coarse and matted, my eyes were dull, my toilet was soft and squidgy. In short, I was a mess. More frightening though, I was only just under a year old and I was dying. Was! That was the most important word. Not any more I'm not.

Over the next couple of days, my condition began to improve noticeably, I began to feel much stronger and more energetic. Christine said that she would like me to live on their terrace where she could keep an eye on me, David agreed but nobody asked me! Their house and terrace are three metres below the track level and accessed by a short flight of steps. Going down these steps in the past, when they had not been there, had made me feel trapped because my escape routes were limited, so now I refused to go. Undeterred David picked me up and carried me down, placing me gently on their terrace.

I stood stock still, I didn't know what to do. David disappeared up the steps again and returned with my crate which he placed in one corner of the terrace. My food and water was placed beside it but, thankfully, I noticed that my way up the steps was not barred so I could walk away whenever I wanted to. I wanted to now so I made a break for it. Two hours of total freedom rejuvenated me and restored my self confidence. I went back down the steps, ate my food and crawled into my shelter to rest. I didn't mind this after all, secure on the terrace but free to come and go.

My attitude changed somewhat when David tied a long blue rope to my collar. I didn't like that one bit, now I was restricted. I felt trapped, I was trapped. Fortunately I only stayed tied up for a couple of days before Christine and David saw sense.

"Why have we tied her up?" Christine questioned. "If any of the wild dogs that live on the mountain come after her the only real defence she has is her speed. Tied up we are taking that away from her."

Not to mention my hard fought freedom.

"That's true." David replied. "But what if she decides to run away?"

"That's her choice."

Yes Christine, got it in one.

If I want to run away it's my choice and I should be able to do so if I want. Then it occurred to me, why would I want to?

The rope disappeared, I didn't. Well not permanently anyway. Each day, after I had devoured my breakfast, I would run off all over the mountain, catching the odd rabbit and generally exploring the area, but I would always return to my crate.

Whenever John and Samson went for their walks I would tag along and Samson and I would catch up on what had been happening. We became very close, so close in fact that sometimes I would go home with him and we would lie on his terrace together. John and Les were great, they spoiled me something rotten and I thought that if I couldn't stay with Christine and David I wouldn't mind staying with Samson, John and Les.

One morning as I lie on my terrace, notice the change of ownership, I heard Samson coming along the track. Great I'll walk with him. I ran up the steps and froze in my tracks, there was another dog walking beside him. She was dark brown, a bit scraggy with hair slightly longer than mine, and whiskers that looked like an old scrubbing brush. I estimated her to be a good four years older than me at least. As I approached Samson looked a little apprehensive.

"Hello girl, this is Rosa, she lives down the track a bit."

"Does she now?"

"Yes my home is about a hundred metres away from Samson's." Rosa's voice was a little deep, butch even, she had an air of smugness about her.

"Is it indeed, well I suggest you trot off back there and leave my Samson alone."

"*Your* Samson? I think not. I have known him since long before you ever stepped paw on this mountain."

"Yes *my* Samson. Now back off or I promise you will regret it."

Rosa grinned pompously and moved closer to Samson. That did it. Enraged I flew at her, determined to wipe that smug grin off her face. She hadn't seen it coming, she was slow and out of condition following years of cosseting, so I caught her off balance with my speed and crashed into her side with my shoulder.

She went sprawling, legs kicking wildly at fresh air. Before she had a chance to regain her feet and her poise I pounced on her and got a tight grip round her throat as if she were a mere rabbit. When she recovered from her initial surprise she wriggled and kicked out at me, trying all the time to shake my vice-like grip. That wasn't going to happen and with every move she made I tightened my death grip another notch. After a couple of minutes rolling in the dust her lips and inside her ears began to change colour, I knew I had her beaten but did she know it? She stopped wriggling, conceding defeat. Gingerly I let her go, all the time watching out for any sign of her renewing the fight but she realised she was well beaten, she had more than met her match. Getting to her feet she glowered at me.

"Goodbye Rosa." I built on my success. With her tail between her legs she walked sadly back to her home, she never made another move for my Samson.

When she had completely disappeared from view I turned to Samson, who had sat down to watch the scrap, obviously pleased to have two girls fighting over him. John just stood there smiling.

I smiled at him, he smiled back and winked at me. I knew from that moment that we were an item.

"C'mon girl, let's walk."

I never did find out exactly what sweetheart meant but apparently it was used as an endearment and was never my real name. Christine had a string of endearments for me, sweetheart, sweetie, poppet and luvvie were just a few of them. One day, as I lie on the kitchen floor, yes I had progressed to going indoors now, I heard her talking to David over breakfast.

"We ought to have a name for her, what do you think of Lucky?" That brought me up sharp.

Oh please no! You can't call me Lucky anything but that it's so naff.

"Don't you think that's a bit crass?" David introduced a bit of common sense to the discussion.

Well done David.

"Mmm possibly, how about Hope then?"

No!

I screamed my disgust, although apparently they couldn't hear me.

That's ten times worse than Lucky, please David, pleeeease.

"Oh no, that's worse, that's really dreadful."

Thank you David.

The telepathy is beginning to work.

S*uggest something serious.*

"OK well I am forever calling her Poppet so how about that for an idea?" Christine continued.

Help!

"Sorry love but if you think that I'm going to take her for a walk calling, Poppet, here Poppet, you have another thought coming."

Reprieve!

"OK so why not change it a bit to Poppy?"

Hum! That sounds alright. I wouldn't mind that.

"Yes that sounds better." Telepathy mode, I can work him easily. "I could go for that."

"Poppy it is then." Christine had a satisfied smile but it wasn't half as big as mine.

The next morning I couldn't wait to tell Samson.

"Hey, you'll never guess, I've got a name. I'm called Poppy now."

"Poppy; Poppy, I like that." I even had the Samson seal of approval. "C'mon Poppy, let's walk."

It looked to me as if my plan to get Christine and David to keep me permanently was beginning to work; already I had a name, which was a promising start. Giving me a name was an acceptance of me being theirs but I just needed a little something to tip the balance a bit more in my favour. I knew just what to do. One afternoon they were sitting on their terrace after a morning of hard work and I decided that the time was right.

There was a large family of rabbits living underneath their terrace and another living under their swimming pool and these two families were at the heart of my plan. One by one I flushed them out of their burrows and all afternoon I chased them around the mountain catching five fair sized ones. I took them and laid them on the terrace, side by side, in an orderly line, then I sat and looked at Christine and David and admired my work inclining my head as a request for approval. They were suitably impressed.

"My goodness Chris," David often shortened her name, "Poppy has caught them as a present for us. Can you believe that?"

"Amazing!" Said Christine.

Elementary!

I never did find out what happened to those five rabbits, my intention was that they should enjoy the same kind of meal that I had been used to all my life. I did hear David ask if he should clean them and put them in the freezer. Why he wanted to clean them I don't know because I had been careful not to drag them through the dirt too much and what this freezer thing was I had no idea.

One thing I am sure of is that my present did not come a day too early. Christine and David were sitting on the terrace that night enjoying a drink, I was lying close by snoozing. Christine put her glass on the table and turned to David.

"We need to make a decision on whether we are going to keep Poppy or not." That got my attention, my radar ears twitched in their direction. This was a conversation I had been looking forward to whilst at the same time dreading. The next few minutes could change my life forever. I forced myself not to react save to open my eyes and look sorrowfully up at them. Sad eyes are so effective with humans.

"I have to consider the cats." Said Christine.

Cats! What cats, I don't see any cats, and why do we have to consider them?

"Of course we do."

"I mean they're small and furry so Poppy might see them as rabbits. I can't put them in danger."

I won't harm them. Promise.

"Then there is the question of carpets, we can't have her peeing all over the place because she isn't housetrained. I don't know if it's too late to try and train her."

"Being used to open spaces how would she react to our small house and virtually no garden?"

Oh no! The arguments seemed to be building up against me.

"OK so why don't we talk to Carolina, get her advice and make up our minds from there." It was Christine who had that brainwave.

I was due another vet appointment a couple of days later and was feeling apprehensive as I was lifted into the car for the journey down the mountain, after all this could be a pivotal moment in my life. Once again I managed to deposit my breakfast in the back of the car, all over the blanket which had thoughtfully been placed for my comfort. Not an auspicious start.

Carolina gave me the once over and pronounced me much recovered, I was, she said, strong enough for the operation.

Excuse me! Operation? What is one of them and why do I need it?

Carolina's assistant Christina led me off to another room full of cages of different sizes. There were large cages along each wall at ground level, some empty and some with dogs in and there were some smaller cages above with cats in. I had not actually come into contact with a cat before so this was to be an education. I stared at the cats as I was being encouraged into one of the larger cages, my lead was removed, yes I had a proper lead by now, and Christina left closing the door softly behind her.

My heart sank to the bottom of my paws, obviously this was it I decided. They had weighed up all the pros and cons about me living with them permanently and it looked as if the cons, including the carpet things and the cats had won the day. I hated those cats. I lie down, totally deflated. I was no longer in charge of my own destiny, all my machinations had been for nothing. Since the day I escaped from the hunter I had been able to determine my own destiny, but now I was incarcerated, helpless, my fate lie in the hands of others, what would become of me?

Later Christina came in, clipped my lead on and led me from the room. We entered another room which was really scary. There was a big flat table made of stainless steel, bright lights, lots of equipment and a strange smell. Instantly I recognised that smell, all animals know it when they encounter it, the smell of death. I struggled as I was lifted up onto the table. Please this can't be happening to me!

Christina had a clipper machine in her hand and she proceeded to shave off a square of fur on my front paw.

What's that for? What are you going to do to me?

Carolina approached me, she was dressed differently, she had a plastic apron on and a silly hat. I was terrified. She had a syringe in her hand. I was petrified with fear. Is this how it would all end?

I shied away from her and attempted to pull my shaven paw away. Gently Carolina and Christina coaxed me.

You don't get round me that easily. Please no.

The needle went into my leg. I felt a bit of a sting. The room began to go all funny. I felt woozy.

No, no, nooooo!

The room grew darker and darker until finally everything went black.

The world slowly got brighter. I couldn't focus my eyes, everything was a blur. My belly hurt. I closed my eyes and went back to sleep.

When I woke up properly I wished I hadn't. There was a sharp pain in my belly, my eyes still wouldn't focus properly and to cap it all I had a thumping headache as well. What were they doing to me? What had they already done to me?

Hang on though; I'm still alive, had they changed their mind at the last minute?

I lie there with all kinds of thoughts washing around in my confused, cloudy mind. Very slowly my vision began to improve, the cotton wool in my head began to disappear. When my eyes cleared I recognised the room. I was back in the cage in the back room of the vet's. The headache was clearing but the pain in my belly continued. Every half hour or so somebody entered the room and came to check on me, I think it was Christina but it might have been Carolina, it might even have been both at different times.

I don't know how long I lie there, I think it was quite some time, but eventually Christina came in and opened the cage door, attached my lead and encouraged me to stand.

"Come on Poppy darling, mum and dad are here to take you home."

What? Mum and dad, who are they? Which home?

I was a bit wobbly on my legs, woolly in my head and my belly still hurt but I managed to stagger into the reception area and there stood Christine and David, my pet humans.

"Here we are." Said Christina. "Safely back with mum and dad." I felt confused, I didn't know which side was up.

Mum and dad, mum and dad? Did that mean that Christine and David were now my mum and dad? Immediately I felt a bit better. I remembered that Boy had called his human dad, Samson too called John and Les mum and dad and they all lived at home together. He had explained to me how you get a mum and dad. Could it be?

Had I won? Were they going to take me home for good? Had the telepathy worked?

Yippeeee!

Ouch I shouldn't have done that.

Dad carefully lifted me into the back of the car, there were extra blankets spread out for me. I lie down, there was no way I was going to try and stand for the journey home in my condition. Home, what a lovely word that is.

Home dad! And don't spare the horses.

I didn't know what that meant but I knew I had heard it somewhere before.

When we arrived home I was taken into the house and there by the front door was a brand new, pristine basket complete with mattress and blanket, just for me. I had arrived, I felt so happy that I lie down and cried with happiness.

It only took me a couple of days of lazing around to recover and as I rested I listened very carefully to the conversations that Christine and David, correction, mum and dad, were having. I learned a lot and it was all good.

Apparently I had been taken to the vet in order to have an operation, that's what they call it when they render you unconscious and cut you open to make changes to your insides. In my case they had taken away all the bits I needed to make puppies which meant that I would never be able to conceive. That was fantastic news for me because I never ever wanted to have puppies, not after seeing what it had done to my own mother. Secondly mum and dad had talked to Carolina about their misgivings over giving me home for good. Apparently it was their other home that was the problem. She had advised them that there would be little chance of me attacking their cats and I would be perfectly safe to have around them.

I could have told you that!

I would be as safe as houses with cats but as far as I was aware they didn't have any so what was their concern.

Their doubts about me being able to live in a small house were also removed by Carolina who had told them that I wouldn't care how big or small the house and garden were as long as they were there and they loved me, I would love them back.

I could have told you that as well.

Finally I was to get my very own passport.

Fantastic! My very own passport. What is a passport?

Whatever it is I'm getting one just as soon as I have had my second rabies vaccination. I didn't realise that would mean another needle in the neck but it was worth it in the end.

The time had now come for mum and dad to go to their other home for three months, wherever that home was, I thought home was here on the mountain. They decided that I should be allowed to run free while they were gone and they arranged for Samson's mum and dad, John and Les to feed and look after me. No problem. Three months close to Samson, I could handle that alright, it suited me down to the ground.

The three months went very quickly. I spent most of my days either chasing rabbits or lying on Samson's terrace with him. If the nights were cool or it was raining John and Les would take me into their home. I had a very comfortable three months thank you very much.

When I say three months that was not quite correct, for one of those weeks John and Les had to go back to Inglan, whatever or wherever that is, and Samson and I had to go into something called a kennel. Come the day we were packed into the back of their big Land Rover Discovery and made the fairly short journey down the mountain, of course I threw up again, some things never change. When we arrived at the kennel we were led through a gate and into a big grass area with a tall wire fence all around it. The grass compound was bordered on two sides by wire cages.

"What do you make of this?" I asked Samson.

"Not to worry Pops, I've been here before. It's just somewhere to eat and sleep until mum and dad come back to collect us." We were fed into the wire cage that was to be our shared home for the week and the door was firmly locked behind us.

"Do we get a chance to run free on the mountain?" I asked rather naively.

"No chance, we are let out twice a day to run around outside the cage on the grass." I was beginning to feel that I would not like it here.

"They will come back for us won't they?"

"They always have done so far. Now, stop being silly, lie down and be quiet I want to snooze."

"Great!"

Samson was correct, that's exactly how it was. Twice a day we were allowed to run around, mind you Samson was not that active and he just mooched around while I ran excited circles around him. We had a small meal in the morning and another one in the evening and that was it. I was bored. I wanted to run at full speed on the mountain, I wanted to hunt a rabbit or two. I did not particularly enjoy that week.

One afternoon we were lying in the cage, it seemed we had been there for a year, when Samson pricked up his ears.

"Listen Popps."

"What?"

"That's dad's car, I'd know that engine anywhere." We stared at the road that wound down into the valley and sure enough after a few seconds John's big black car swept round a bend and into view.

"We're going home Pops." Now you have to remember that I was still young and that, having had all the tics removed, I was now full of energy. Coupled with this I had been incarcerated in this wire cage for a week and was feeling rather constrained. I was eager to be free again. Samson and I were released from our cage into the grass area and we ran eagerly toward the main gate and Les, John was not there. Samson was keen to see his mum again and I was desperate for a bit of freedom.

When the owner of the kennel unlocked the gate he either thought that I was easily controlled or his security was a bit lax. In any event I saw a gap between his legs and the gate that I knew I could squeeze through and before anybody had a chance to move I was through his legs and away up the mountain at full speed, with a cloud of dust chasing me up the hillside. The panicked cries of 'Poppy' rapidly fading behind me.

Free again I quartered the hillside searching for a rabbit scent, always keeping Samson, Les and the frustrated but embarrassed kennel owner within sight. I had no intention of running off permanently, I just wanted some freedom for a while. I found a scent easily and had great fun chasing the juvenile to ground, a tasty morsel for breakfast. My jaunt lasted for over an hour, then I looked down to the kennel to where Les was standing, hands on hips. She had long since stopped calling me and so I decided to show off a little by running close to her, close enough to arouse in her the prospect that she might catch me but distant enough to know that she wouldn't be able to.

I enjoyed that close flypast so I decided to do it again, and again. Suddenly on my third or fourth pass a scent wafted up my nostrils and swirled round my millions of smell sensors. It wasn't rabbit, it was much tastier than that, it was chicken. I stopped just out of reach and sniffed the air. Definitely chicken. Les had a large piece of cooked chicken skin in her hand, I love chicken skin. Slowly I crept toward her and very gently took the chicken in my mouth, as I did so her other hand grasped my collar firmly and I was once more a captive. Les was very pleased with herself for catching me but in all honesty I was feeling ready to go home and I was about to give myself up before the chicken skin was offered. Result!

Les had the last laugh though as on the way home I not only brought up the half chewed chicken treat, I also deposited the partly digested rabbit on the floor of her Discovery, so I didn't get to really enjoy either. Samson gave me a firm look of disapproval both for running off and for soiling the back of his car. Mind you, did Les really get the last laugh after all she was the one who had to clean up the mess. Either way I got a great big cuddle from Les when we finally got home so she obviously didn't hold any animosity toward me for my antics.

When our three months enforced separation was over mum and dad returned to their home on the mountain and I reverted to living with them. Being the only non human was good, I began to take over without them realising what was going on. I was happily going into the house and wandering through all the rooms and in the evenings I was most pleased to lie on the sofa with my head on dad's knee as we watched television together. I had even taken to sleeping on the square of carpet in the hallway every night, I had my nice new sleeping basket but being used to the wild I never quite got the hang of using it.

Mum and dad stayed in my home for three weeks and during that time I had to have a couple more injections before I was finally the proud owner of my very own passport. What is a passport? I still don't know what it is, all I know is that I had one of my very own.

The three weeks passed very quickly and before I knew it the time had come for mum and dad to catch the plane back to this Inglan place.

Can I come too?

No such luck. I was taken back to the kennel place, on my own this time, and I watched as dad's car slipped down the road into the dry river bed, up the other side, climbed up the winding road and disappeared out of view round the bend. I was desolate. I cried. I was locked into my wire cage all alone. Crestfallen I crept into the covered area at the back, slumped down on the floor and cried myself to sleep. I felt so low, how could they leave me here again, alone, how long was I destined to be here this time? Maybe three months until they returned again? This was no life I thought, not what I had expected or hoped for, perhaps I should reconsider my future. Of course I was not privy to the arrangements that had been made, if I had been I would have understood what was happening to me. I found out later that mum and dad went in a plane which went in the sky to take them to their other home in this Inglan place that I kept hearing about. Being a dog, I was not allowed in this plane apparently.

Exactly one week later I heard what I knew to be dad's car engine. I couldn't believe my ears, he was back so soon. I bounded up to the gate of my cage and stared to where I knew the road emerged from the bend, sure enough, seconds later, dad's car came sweeping round, down the winding road, through the dry river bed and up to the kennel. He disappeared into the office. It seemed an age before he emerged and approached the main gate. The kennel owner released me from my cage and I ran, as fast as my legs could carry me, up to my dad. This time I had no desire to make a break I was so pleased to see him. At the back of my mind I had still maintained a nagging feeling that I was going to be abandoned again, but those thoughts quickly evaporated when I saw the great big grin on his face.

I had not been fed that morning, it seemed dad had finally realised that cars and a full stomach did not go together well with me, so for once I did not puke in the back of the car. When we arrived home I raced down the steps to see mum, she wasn't there to greet me. Dad unlocked the house, swiftly I searched every room, they were all empty, mum was nowhere to be seen.

What's going on? Where's mum?

"Just a couple of days to rest and then we're going home to England together." Dad said.

But where's mum?

"Mum is looking after our cats and waiting for us to get back." Telepathy restored to working order again without him realising what was happening.

The next day dad went out in the car and returned with a big cardboard box, I was inquisitive. From within the box he drew a flat wire thing, I say thing because at that time I had no idea what it could be. He unfolded it, lifted the top, pulled up the sides, I was intrigued and when he had done, hey presto, there was a big wire cage. He slipped the cage into the back of the car, a blanket and an old sleeping bag were laid out on the bottom and suddenly it all became clear to me. This cage was for me to sleep in during the journey. It must be a long journey, I wonder how long it will take.

A wonderful realisation hit me. If mum and dad were going to all this trouble and expense, I was definitely now an integral part of the family. I had done it. I had my new loving home.

Whoo hooo!!

The next morning dad got up quite early, had his breakfast and pitched his overnight bag into the car. Also into the car went a cooler box of food and drink and a handful of CD's. Lastly I was carefully lifted and placed into the wire cage. I put on my mystified look. Dad rubbed my ears, stroked my head and gave me a big kiss on the side of my snout.

"We're on our way Popps." A last tickle behind the ear and another kiss, dad closed and latched the wire door on the cage and closed the tailgate of the car.

We swept down the undulating mountain road until we reached the roundabout at the bottom where the road joined the motorway.

"Cross the roundabout, second exit, then turn left."
Who said that?

I sat up straight, ears in radar mode. Dad was on his own but that was definitely a female human voice. We safely negotiated the first roundabout.

"Cross the roundabout, third exit, then join the motorway."

There it was again, where is she? Who is she?

Dad swung round the roundabout and charged up the on slip.

"Join the motorway."

Who? Where? What?

We joined the motorway and I listened intently for the voice to come again, I would soon detect the source. For kilometre after kilometre we drove but the voice remained ominously silent. Whoever it had been must have gone away I concluded. I lie down and looked out the rear window to see where we were had come from. Eventually my eyelids became heavy and I slipped close to sleep.

"Junction ahead."

She's back. I leapt to my feet and stared over dad's shoulder, radar at the ready.

"In five hundred metres keep right." Got it, she was inside a little box attached to the dashboard.

How did she get in there? The box was very small so either she is a very small person or it's magic. There was a picture on the box too, and it moved.

"Keep right then take the motorway." Yep she was definitely in that box but who she was and why she was there goodness only knew. She kept telling dad which direction he should go and I realised that she must be some sort of talking map, but who she was I had no idea until, having been told to 'turn around when possible', dad finally let the secret out.

"Thank you Digital Doris." He sounded a tad irritated. Why would he want to turn around? I was the only thing in the back of the car and I was behaving perfectly, there was no reason for him to turn around and check on me. In any case, shouldn't he concentrate on where he was going, it would be dangerous to turn around. At least I knew her name now, Digital Doris, strange name though.

Every two or three hours dad stopped so that he could have something to eat or drink, stretch his legs, go to the toilet or put more fuel in the car. I was lifted out of the cage so that I could have a little walk too, on a lead of course, which enabled me to relieve the stiffness in my legs and have a pee of my own.

The journey was long, all day we drove, the world outside the car changed from the dry brown scorched landscape to a more lush green, the kind I had never laid eyes on before. Eventually the sky darkened and the stars came out, dad turned bright eyes on in the front of the car so he could see where we were going, still we continued.

When it got really late dad pulled into a rest area and we stretched our legs, peed and had some refreshment, I only had a little water and a couple of biscuits during the whole day, cars and food don't go well with me you remember. When dad climbed back into the car he locked the doors, pulled out a pillow and a blanket, wrapped himself up and curled up to sleep. 'Wow' I thought this must be a long journey. I circled around in my cage for two or three turns, to trample the imaginary grass, before plonking myself down, snorting, letting out a deep sigh and settling down to sleep.

I was awoken by dad moving about. It was still pitch black outside and I estimated that we had only slept for three or four hours. Dad stowed the pillow and blanket and slipped out of the car. A waft of chill air flooded in, it was unusually cold outside, well unusually for me anyway. He flexed his legs and stamped his feet for a bit, adjusted his trousers, why do men always do that, and then he climbed back into the car.

"Time to hit the road again Popps." With that he gunned the engine, selected first gear and we were off again.

"In two hundred metres take the motorway."

Oh shut up Doris!

We drove again for almost the whole day, this mysterious Inglan must be a long way from my mountain. I watched as the sky began to lighten, a thin pink band emerged from the ground, growing bigger and redder as it did so, dawn was breaking over the countryside. The redness disappeared as clouds started to roll in and the sun disappeared. The day was again punctuated with the usual food, fuel and pee stops but we also paused at a number of small houses and dad gave the person inside the house some money. I remember thinking that was very generous of him, these people could only afford a kennel sized home and he was helping them by giving them money.

As daylight began to fade once more into night we arrived at a strange place. It was like a big car park but nobody was parked. Dad joined the end of a queue of cars and edged toward another small house, similar to the ones he had given money to but about twice the size. When it was his turn he took a paper out of a folder and handed it to the man in the house. They talked of boats and times and then the man asked if dad had any pets.

"Yes, just the one dog." He replied. The man handed him a thing like a table tennis bat and dad made his way to the back of the car. He opened the cage and waved this bat around near my neck, it beeped.

Nice trick dad.

The bat was handed back to the man and he gave dad some new papers. We drove off and joined the back of another queue. Engine off dad climbed out and lifted me to the ground. We went for a fairly long walk. The air smelled different. I stopped, pointed my nose to the sky and sniffed. I detected salty air, we were near the sea. I also detected oil, rubber, people and rubbish. I wondered where we could be.

It wasn't long before I found out. We rejoined the car and dad picked his mobile and phoned mum.

"Hi sweetheart .... Yes made good time....just at Calais waiting for the boat ..... Yes of course I will .... OK sweetheart .... Love you ... bye."

So now I knew we were at a place called Calais waiting for a boat, but where Calais was and what a boat was I had no idea so I was no further forward really. When the queue eventually began to move we were directed up a concrete ramp. At the top of the ramp there was a big entrance into something that looked like a garage except that everything was made of metal, metal walls, metal roof and metal floor. All the cars that had been in front of us in the queue were parked in lines, we were directed to our line and then other cars came right up behind us, it was impossible to drive out because we were completely boxed in.

Dad got out of the car, made a fuss of me and told me he would be back soon and that I should be a good girl. Then he disappeared through a doorway and was gone. All the people from all the other cars disappeared through the same doorway, it must be a very big room on the other side! I was apprehensive, I was alone in the car and people were walking all about heading for that doorway. I barked but evidently dad didn't hear me because he didn't come back, he usually came when I called. I barked at the people for a couple of minutes to keep them away from the car but decided that it was pointless, nobody took any notice of me and nobody was interested in the car. At least I was in the car so I knew dad would come back to me when he could. I made myself comfortable and closed my eyes.

Whoa! What was that?

The floor was moving and all the cars with it. There was a throbbing vibration which grew more intense. Yes, the garage was definitely moving. After a while the vibration grew even stronger and the garage started to rock, I was confused and just a bit frightened. Fortunately it wasn't too long, maybe only a couple of hours, before the rocking stopped and the vibration diminished. Loads of people flooded out of the doorway, including dad, and I began to feel a whole lot better.

"OK Popps, once we get off this boat it's motorway almost all the way home."

Ah so this metal garage must be a boat. When dad drove out of the garage everything had changed. The ramp was different, the car park was different, the buildings were different; how did that happen?

We followed a line of cars, winding round the car park, through a shed where uniformed people waved at us, that was nice of them, and out onto a motorway.

Careful dad you are driving on the wrong side of the road. Mind you so is everybody else!

Digital Doris made no mention of it so I assumed it must be alright, if a bit weird.

I turned to look out of the rear window, we were climbing up a hill and I could plainly see the car park we had driven across. I could see the metal garage, the same shape as some wooden ones I had seen from the hills at home, but much bigger. I realised that must be a boat, we had been on that boat and crossed a sea. Wow, this Inglan place was a long way from home.

After a couple of hours on the road we arrived at a big town and dad drove the car into a small street with houses down each side, it was like nothing I had ever seen before. Dad parked the car by some green grass, I thought grass was always brown, and I was liberated from my cage. I was led toward a house at the end of a row of four. As we approached, the door opened and there stood mum with her arms open wide. She gave big hugs, first to dad and then to me, and ruffled my ears.

"You had better come in and meet the rest of the family Poppy."

Meet the rest of the family? The REST of the family.

It's official I'm part of the family.

I went inside the house; it was small and cosy with soft stuff on the floors, all the floors, that must be this carpet stuff that they thought I might damage. There was a sitting room with a couple of sofas, a table and two chairs, and a small kitchen. A wide door led from the back into a small garden.

It all seemed so strange to me. Cautiously I stepped through the front door and came face to face with a furry creature. He was mostly white with a few dark grey blotches, small pointy ears, a small pink nose, soft lemon eyes and long whiskers.

"Hello Poppy." He said with a warm smile on his face. "We have been waiting to meet you, mum has told us all about you. I'm Ollie, and that over there is Simba." I turned my head in the direction he pointed and saw another fluffy creature lying hunched up. She was brown and black with touches of white on her feet and she eyed me with dark suspicious eyes for a few seconds before turning and running upstairs.

"You will have to be a little bit careful with Simba." Ollie warned. "She doesn't like anyone but herself and she can be a bit vicious."

"Oh OK!" I was a little shell-shocked, everything was so different to home.

"You'll love it here though, nice and cosy, mum and dad are great and make a fuss of us all." I decided that I liked Ollie, he was so cheerful and friendly.

"I take it that you are one of the cats that I have heard so much about."

"Got it in one. I'm a cat and proud of it. Sometimes called a kitty, or a puss or even a bugger if I accidentally catch dad with my claws or almost trip him up by walking in front of him."

"You look so different to the cats back home, they are mostly thin with pointy faces and short hair."

"I suppose that's because we need more fur and food to keep us warm in the cold winter months."

"I think you may be right." I sniffed him a bit by way of introduction, just to be friendly and he sniffed me in return. "You know that they thought I might chase you and kill you, don't you?"

"Yeah! Humans eh! What do they know?" I walked into the sitting room and looked about. "Sit wherever you like mate we don't stand on ceremony here."

From that moment on Ollie and I were the greatest of buddies, we would often sit together and talk. Sometimes he would lick my head or my ears and sometimes I would lick him. During our chats he asked me how I came to be with mum and dad. He was not surprised when I told him that I had effectively been dying as a stray when mum and dad took pity on me. He confided that he had been taken in as a stray too, as indeed had Simba.

"I think," he mused, "that dad was a stray taken in by mum too."

I asked him to tell me his story, he smiled.

"Not as eventful as yours Pop."

When a neighbour living in an adjacent road had moved away they decided that they didn't want to take him with them so they put him out on the street and left. In his search for some shelter, and a place that he could call home, he had been accosted by a gang of children who taunted and chased him. Every time they saw him they threw stones at him and chased him away. Finally he had been attacked by a vicious dog, that the owner failed to control properly, and in the ensuing fight he had a lump bitten out of his neck.

"That made me very wary of humans, especially children, and dogs." He explained. "So I spread my search a bit wider until one day I happened on the garden next door." I had seen that 'garden' and the word was applicable only in the extremely loosest of terms. It was more like a jungle, all brambles, long grass and stinging nettles.

"I was grateful though," he continued, "it gave me the security I needed. No children or dogs would venture into that mass of thorns. There was someone who discovered me though."

"I hope they didn't hurt you."

"No way, it was Sophie, who lived here at the time, she became the closest friend I have ever had in my life. She would lie beside me in the nettles and brambles and keep me company all day."

"What happened to Sophie?"

"She was a beautiful cat, you would have loved her, she was my soul mate and dad loved her to bits, which says something seeing as he is really a dog person. Sadly she was taken ill a couple of months ago and died soon after. Everybody loved her, I know I did."

"That's very sad. Sorry I didn't mean to interrupt you."

"That's alright. One day when mum was looking for Sophie she discovered me with her and after that she kept leaving food and water out for me. Gradually she encouraged me out of the brambles so I let her tickle my nose as a reward. After that my food was put on the ground just inside the garden where the fence has a sort of cat flap, to encourage me out of the brambles. From there I progressed to sitting on the roof of their shed where I could see into the house."

As if he were reliving the experience, he sighed and there was a long pause before he continued.

"There were four cats here then, every one a stray. There was Sophie as I said, then there was Pippa who was an outside cat and would never go in the house. The other two were Amber and Max."

"Are they still here?"

"Sadly no. Three years ago Amber developed kidney failure and, although mum tried everything, she could not be saved and she died in mums arms."

"That's very sad."

"Mum cried for days because Amber was rather a favourite of hers. Unfortunately though worse was to come. The following week Max died after being hit by a car. That was when I decided that mum needed someone else to love so I decided to move in."

"How did you manage to swing that?"

"Mum went to work and dad left the back door open, I came in and refused to go out for three weeks until I was sure that they wouldn't get rid of me."

"This is a bit of a home for strays isn't it."

"Certainly is, as I said even dad is a stray apparently, so Sophie told me. She fell in love with him and let him stay."

"Sophie or mum?"

"Both of them."

This was obviously a very kind house, everything felt warm and homely; I knew I would enjoy it here. I was well fed and putting on weight and would soon be where I should be, my fighting weight you might say. I was allowed to sit on the sofa, sometimes of an evening I would sit with dad as he watched football on television or I would sit with mum as she did some knitting. I even sat on the sofa during the day if I was not in the garden that is.

When the time came to go to bed I was allowed on the sofa on my own with a blanket placed over me, whilst mum, dad, Ollie and Simba went upstairs to bed. Technically speaking Simba didn't go upstairs she was already there, in fact she was almost a permanent fixture up there.

When I first arrived in the house she had been sitting on the bottom of the stairs, she took one look at me and bolted upstairs. She stayed up there for four days without venturing downstairs at all, not even to use the dirt tray, that's where cats poo and pee, they don't have to go outside like I do. That's unfair when it is raining. But I digress.

I heard Ollie telling her that it was safe and that I would not hurt her but all she did was hiss at him and tell him to go away.

In the end, because she had been up in the bedroom for so long without visiting the toilet tray, which was downstairs, she wet the bed. Ollie came bounding down and whispered to me.

"Watch out Popp there is going to be an explosion when mum discovers what Simba has done." He was wrong, of course mum wasn't very pleased, that's an understatement, but she understood that Simba had not been in close proximity to a dog before and she was frightened to venture downstairs. She just said to dad that they needed to get a new mattress and bedding anyway so this had just brought forward the purchase.

Next time mum and dad went out I crept upstairs and into the bedroom. Simba eyed me with hostile suspicion. She hissed.

"Come on Simba." I said. "Don't be afraid of me, I will never hurt you, I would like to be your friend."

"Me; a friend to a dog. Never." She hissed again.

"What's wrong, why do you hate dogs so?"

"I don't hate just dogs, I hate cats, rabbits, mice and most humans too. I hate you, now go away and leave me alone."

Well that's cleared that up then! I couldn't leave her like that so I stayed by the open door and talked to her in the softest tones I could manage.

"You're wasting your time." Ollie shouted up the stairs.

"You're not helping Ollie, why don't you have a sleep on the window sill?"

It took quite some time but eventually I got Simba to open up to me, just a little. She told me that when she was a kitten she had lived with a family a couple of streets away, they had named her 'Biscuit' because of her colouring which was similar to a digestive biscuit, she is actually a Burmese Cross, so called I believe because she is Burmese and permanently cross. The two children in the family had treated her very roughly, pulling her tail, picking her up by her front legs, dangling her by her back legs, locking her in cupboards and generally being cruel to her. One day she had snapped and had clawed at the little boy who had just singed her whiskers with his father's cigarette lighter. She was kicked by the father and thrown out, literally, thrown out of the kitchen window.

She had been on her own since then but because she was different from the rest of the cats in the street they also turned on her and scratched her.

All the dogs chased her continually so she ran away. She arrived at mum and dad's house and sensed the love so she came in. She was chased out, mum threw a bowl of water at her and dad sprayed her with a garden hose because they wanted to discourage her, after all they had three cats already. Simba had persevered and mum and dad had eventually relented and accepted her.

"I know that they don't really want me either." She said sadly. "But I've nowhere else to go. So...." She tailed off with a tear in her eye. I knew instinctively that she was wrong. Mum and dad loved her too. We talked some more and I think that I eventually convinced her that she was the same as us, she agreed to be more friendly.

"Not too friendly though." She smiled. "I've got my reputation to protect you know."

From that moment on Simba became more friendly to everybody, she just didn't let it show that's all.

The garden in Inglan was very small, so small in fact that I could not get to stretch my legs properly unless I was chasing a squirrel. Trouble was by the time I reached full speed it was time to stop and I often banged my nose on the wooden fence because I couldn't stop quickly enough. Dad got over this lack of exercise by taking me for a walk on some nearby meadows every morning. He would put on a warm coat and big walking boots and if the weather was really cold he donned a woolly hat and scarf before attaching me to my new lead. It was a special lead, if he pressed a button I could walk or run quite a long way from him. The first time I did it I didn't realise that there was actually a maximum distance I could go from dad so I ran off and was brought up very sharply as the lead went taut and my head turned sideways, I think dad's arm almost came out of its socket too. Now I know the exact length of the lead I rarely jolt dad's arm.

We walk along the road for a while before turning into a narrow lane, that is where I always hear the click that tells me the lead has been released and I have my five metres of freedom.

While on the extended lead I can go into hedges, between trees and under bushes to have a really good sniff around.

One of the first things that struck me about Inglan was that all of the smells were different to those I had become accustomed to on the mountain. Damp grass and the dew on leaves smelled so sweet and fresh. Branches that had broken off trees smelled of rot and decay whereas the trees themselves smelled of rising sap and musty bark.

There was different wildlife too, instead of the geckos, lizards and snakes that I was used to there were mice, voles, snails, slugs and earthworms. I don't like snails and slugs ugh! Interestingly there were lots of different birds too but I never get anywhere near them, they cheat and fly off. I have promised myself that one day I will catch a pigeon. There was also my familiar and favourite quarry, rabbits. I recognised their scent immediately, it was exactly the same as the rabbits back home.

I also found a new quarry to chase, squirrels. They always stank of stale pee so I could detect them from a long way away, horrible things squirrels, one whiff of them and I was desperate to show them who is boss.

Normally the walks dad and I took should have lasted for about an hour and a half and cover around five kilometres, but this was not the case in the beginning, and that was completely down to me alone. Nobody we encountered had ever seen a Podenco Andaluz before and the other dog walkers would stop to talk to dad. The conversation would usually go like this.

"What a gorgeous dog."

Naturally! How observant you are.

"Thank you." Dad always smiled at this point.

"What breed is he?"

Excuse me but I'm a she.

"She's a Podenco Andaluz."

"A what?"

"A Podenco Andaluz. she's a Spanish hunting dog, originally bred from the Egyptian Pharaoh dog, and used to hunt rabbits and small mammals."

Then they would make a fuss of me and ask dad more questions. I didn't mind that at first but after a couple of months I got a bit bored being the centre of attraction all the time.

Why don't you put a label round my neck dad?

One day, though, dad got a bit worried when a police car passed us and the officer in the passenger seat gave us both a steely stare. The car turned round and crept along the kerb until it reached us.

"Excuse me sir." I felt dad tense, he couldn't think what was coming and I don't think policemen are dad's favourite people somehow. "What kind of dog is that?" Oh my goodness, here we go again. Dad explained, the policeman paid me compliments and then went on his way. I could feel dad relax.

I always keep a keen eye out for squirrels on our walks and as we stroll down the lane toward the meadows I constantly dart from side to side with my eyes focussed firmly on the trees above. I know that I can't catch them when they are up so high but that doesn't stop me trying. One warm summer's day mum decided to come on our walk with us. There had been heavy rain the night before so there were lots of puddles on the lane and the dirt footpaths.

I don't like getting my feet wet or dirty, I have my pride, so I always walk around puddles. This day was no different.

About a quarter of an hour into the walk we stroll down a beautiful dirt bridle way, which is known as 'Oak Lane' because it has rows of oak trees on either side. In the autumn we love to kick up all the golden leaves. At the bottom of the lane, before we actually come out onto the meadows, there is a section where we cross over a bridge spanning a reasonably sized brook. Sometimes I have a swim here, on very rare occasions when the day is particularly hot. Well not actually a swim, I don't swim, but I wade in and stand for a couple of minutes before coming out and soaking dad as I shake off the excess water. After the bridge the track winds round a corner, over a narrow drainage ditch and out into the open meadow.

On this particular day we were approaching the ditch when I spied a squirrel low down in a tree beside the footpath. He was definitely low enough for me to reach, if I were quick enough. With my eyes locked on the furry quarry and all my concentration firmly focussed on him I was completely oblivious to everything else around me, and I mean everything.

When the time was right I leapt into action, literally, I sprang toward the tree he was sitting in which was only two strides away, but my leap was not as I expected. When I made that first bound I expected my paws to make contact with earth again so that I could make my second leap, not so. My feet failed to make any contact at all and I felt as if I was flying, but flying in a downward direction.

Before I had fully realised the situation I landed in the bottom of the ditch, up to my waist in smelly black mud. I squelched into the sticky mass and my legs disappeared. I was up to my chin in the foul goo. Struggle as I might I could not escape the sucking gunge. Dad pulled on my lead but it made no impression, I was stuck fast. In the end dad had to climb down into the ditch and manhandle me out of the mess, we were both covered in the filthy stuff.

Dad went back to the stream and washed his arms and did his best to encourage me into the water to wash off the thick black goo, but I was having none of it, the water was much too cold for me and after all it was wet too, remember I don't do wet! I completed my walk looking embarrassingly filthy, unable to hold my head up but with a gathering crust round my nether region.

Since then I have found that there is a secluded spot further round the walk, a small wooden bridge crosses the stream where it is at its narrowest. The water is usually up to my back but on a hot day I like to hop into the water and just stand there, every time it reminds me of that day when I stood in the water trough in the unfriendly village, the memory somehow makes me appreciate what I have all the more. If it is really warm I might walk around a bit but I never swim and I am never in the water for more than a couple of minutes.

Some days we don't go for a walk at all or we go for a quick walk around the local streets and this is because of one thing, rain! I don't like rain, if at all possible I will stay firmly indoors until it stops.

Normally, if mum and dad want me to go to the toilet they open the back door and I trot off into the garden to do what must be done. If, however, it is raining I will poke my nose out of the door, detect the rain, and come straight back in. I will hold on as long as is caninely possible before I go, and often dad has to push me outside against my will.

Unwilling to get myself wet on a meadow walk, therefore, we have to wait until the rain eases to a fine drizzle when I will allow dad to quickly walk me round the streets.

Going back to the meadow walks, on another occasion I surprised quite a few people, including dad, with a fantastic display of speed. On the meadows I can smell rabbit continually because there are so many of them about, the air and ground is thick with their odour, they must come out in force at night. This particular morning I was happily strolling along when I got a stronger than usual whiff of rabbit. Instinctively I knew that I was very close to one of my furry adversaries and suspected that it had sensed my presence and was lying low hoping that, like many dogs native to Inglan, I would just pass by. I however, am not a native of Inglan, I don't pass up a chance to chase rabbit.

I stayed close to dad, a little behind him so that his scent would mask mine and the rabbit would smell and sense him rather than me, I had my nose about a paws width above the ground. We came very close to him, in fact we were only about two or three metres away, when the rabbit finally lost his nerve, either he caught a whiff of me or, more likely, he thought dad was coming a bit too close. He jumped up and made a break for safety but rather than just run directly away he decided to cross our path. Bad decision, I was far too quick for him, rabbits in Inglan are too fat to be fast runners. The extending lead gives me five metres from dad's arm but before I had reached its maximum extent I had the rabbit under my paws. He struggled but I wrapped my powerful jaws around his chest and his fate was sealed.

A number of other dog walkers stared at me, some in awe of my speed and some no doubt feeling sorry for the rabbit. I lie with my paws across his motionless chest and looked up at dad.

Can I take it home for mum?

"Good girl Popps, you were like lightning."

I took that to mean yes, so I picked up the fat old rabbit in my lethal jaws and continued proudly on the walk. We were only half way round the meadows so I had about two and a half kilometres to carry him and he was a big boy, that had probably slowed him down too, but let's not take any of the credit away from me. His lollopy head almost touched the ground on one side of my mouth and his hind legs tussled the tops of the blades of grass as I proudly pranced along. Once or twice, as I returned home in triumph, even my powerful jaws began to ache and I had to put him down for a short while, but eventually I made it home and placed his floppy form on the doorstep for mum to inspect.

Dad took me inside for a well earned rest and a welcome drink of water whilst mum stepped out to examine my handiwork. She was suitably impressed with my present and made a great fuss of me, but I never did find out exactly what had happened to it, I never saw it again. I hope and expect that he was the main ingredient in the stew that dad had the next day.

My hunting prowess was not only confined to our walks I was pretty good in the garden too. As I have already said the garden was fairly small and was bordered by a metal fence on two sides and a wooden fence on the other. There is a large tree at the bottom of the garden which often has squirrels sitting in it, despite my barking at them, and a dead tree trunk nearer the house which mum uses to hang bird feeders on.

Bird feeders attract birds, obviously, but they also attract squirrels who show off by hanging upside down and stealing the peanuts. If I am indoors, and I see a squirrel on the feeders, I bark and jump up at the door. Unable to bear my exuberant behaviour either mum or dad will open the door for me and I can chase the little rodents out of the garden. They run along the metal fence and either scamper up the big tree or, more often than not, leap into next door's garden. I don't like that because when they are safe they stop and make fun of me, sitting conveniently out of reach on a branch, gnawing at a nut.

There was one squirrel in particular, I called him 'lucky', oh how I hated him, I had chased him many times but he always stayed just out of reach as he scampered round the boundary fence, then he would sit on a branch, as close to me as he safely could, and taunt me. I swear he would stick his tongue out at me. Little ******. I vowed that one day I would wipe that smirk off his stupid face.

That day arrived, it was a Friday, I remember particularly because mum and dad had been early morning shopping and dad was preparing bacon rolls for breakfast, their Friday ritual when in Inglan. Lucky was sitting above the bird feeder nibbling nuts in that hurried nervous way that squirrels have. Mum opened the door in answer to my bark, I charged outside and made a bee line for the rotten rodent. He saw me coming and turned to run along the top of the fence. As he did so he lost his footing on the smooth metal top and plummeted to the ground landing on his feet and literally hitting the ground running as the humans say. He set off hot foot across the grass heading for the big tree and safety. Squirrels are notoriously quick creatures but a Podenco is even quicker, I was on him before he got half way across the grass. Anxious to avoid his razor sharp claws I grabbed his head in my mouth and a swift shake was all it took, I heard the crack as his neck snapped and I let him slip to the ground. I looked down on his inert body. Not so lucky now are we, you smug tree rat.

"Just going to the shops, we won't be long." Now that is a saying mum and dad always use and if they think that they are fooling anybody they are seriously mistaken. What they actually mean is that they are simply going out without us. Whether that is to visit friends, going to a bar or restaurant for a meal, going to the doctor's, in fact going anywhere. Sometimes, although rarely, it really does mean that they are going shopping.

So one day, all dressed up neatly in their going out clothes, mum and dad trotted out that favourite phrase as they headed for the front door. Ollie and I just looked knowingly at each other.

Whatever.

However, before they had a chance to leave, the window cleaner came whistling down the pathway. Mum had wanted the windows cleaned for a while so they decided to postpone their excursion for half an hour and wait while he cleaned all of the windows, packed up his ladder, accepted his payment and departed.

"Right." Said dad. "You had better go busy." That was another favourite word that they use all the time, what it means is that they want me to go outside to toilet of either type, as if I require encouragement to go, unless it is raining of course. Having said the magic word, he opened the back door for me and out I trotted. I skipped down the garden and had a delicious pee and turned to return to the house. It was at this point that I noticed that the window cleaner had neglected to close the garden gate. A good opportunity for me to do a bit of unrestrained exploration I thought. Casually, not wishing to be noticed, I walked out of the gate and into the street. I wandered around the trees undetected until I heard dad shout an expletive. He came rushing out of the garden gate and spied me about twenty five metres away.

"Poppy! Good girl. Poppy come!" He called.

'Poppy explore' was what the little voice inside said. I ran off toward the main road with dad puffing heavily in hot persuit.

"God no! The main road."

Yes I know I'm not stupid.

I ran across the busy main road, easily avoiding the speeding cars, and into a wooded area on the other side, dad followed me over the road and plunged into the undergrowth after me. The wood had a natural slope into a kind of valley which had a layer of thick sticky black mud in the bottom that reached half way up to dad's knees. I know that for a fact because whereas I leapt easily over the mud dad, unfortunately, sank with a squidgy sound. I ran along the bottom of the valley with dad squelching along behind, slurping with each step as he dragged his feet free of the mud only for them to squidge back. Considerately I waited for dad to almost catch me up before I bounded off again under a thicket of brambles. Dad finally managed to extricate himself from the mud and plunged into the brambles after me, calling me continually, and not just my name either. This was a good game, I was having fun.

At the bottom of the hill I bounded out of the wood and re-crossed the main road, a car horn behind told me that dad was still following. This side of the road had a small thicket of trees and bushes with houses beyond, houses were a different proposition to me and I ran around them for a while before getting bored. I stood still amid some rose bushes in somebody's front garden and waited for dad to catch up. It took him a few minutes to appear but eventually he plodded round the corner and looked me straight in my eyes. He was puffing.

Hello dad, you made it then.

He was coated in mud up to his knees but amazingly he was smiling. I took pity on him and walked slowly up to him and sat down. He sat down beside me with a tired bump and gripped my collar.

"You're a sod, do you know that Popps?"

Yeah but you love me dad.

In his haste to follow me he had neglected to bring a lead and his stiff back prevented him from walking beside me bent over. Without another thought he put one arm under my bum and the other under my neck and lifted me up. I weigh around twenty five kilogrammes, that's as much as a bag of cement, but dad carried me all the way home, nuzzling his face into my side and telling me I was a good girl to have come back to him.

Mum made a fuss of me when I got home. Simba gave me a look which said I was very naughty while Ollie just gave me a cheeky smile.

"Welcome home Popps, enjoy your trip?" I returned his smile.

Dad had to have a shower and change all his clothes before, eventually, they made it to the shops. Strangely that night dad didn't go far he just dozed off in front of the television. Can't think why.

That was not the only time I went walkabout in Inglan on my own. Next time it was dad and not the window cleaner who made it all possible. Mum and dad had installed a child gate at the door between the hallway and the lounge in order to make sure that I could not sneak out, especially if they had to answer the front door to a caller. On this particular day dad thought that he had latched the gate correctly but in fact he hadn't. I was quick to notice the mistake. When he opened the front door, and his attention was on the caller, I moved slowly towards him and, taking advantage of his distraction, I pushed quickly between his legs, out of the door and away.

Frantically dad called after me but his voice grew fainter and fainter as I made a top speed break for the main road. I charged down to the bottom of the hill eager to explore a bit further than I had on my previous unescorted excursion. There I discovered another similar wooded area except that this one did not have the mud nor the brambles, what it did have was a number of rough footpaths winding in and out of the trees. I ploughed into the trees with dad nowhere in sight, just a faint voice chasing after me. I roamed around a bit, sniffing here and there without finding any scent that interested me, until I noticed that a van had stopped and two young men had got out. They were talking to a puffing dad and had obviously seen him chasing after me and decided to help him. That was a nice thought.

I also noticed that a neighbour had followed dad in her car, she too was eager to help. This was brilliant, I was the undoubted focus of everybody's attention, and they were all trying to catch little old innocent me. I was having great fun and was keen to make it even more exciting. I stopped to look behind me just as dad plunged into the thicket.

I decided to up the fun stakes a notch. I made sure that dad could see me most of the time, just to taunt him and then I ran along a footpath. Two or three times I ran to within a couple of metres of him and when he was poised to make a lunge for me I would veer away, staying tantalisingly just out of reach. The two young men from the van were on my trail too so I let them think that they had cornered me before running past them at full speed.

Can't catch me!

Dad's face was beginning to turn an attractive shade of red and he was blowing heavily, after all at sixty two he was not as fit as he had been, so I slowed down just enough to let him catch his breath and think he could get hold of me before running away again.

I kept up this cat and mouse chase, or rather dog and human chase, for over half an hour. By this time the two young men had given up, made their excuses and left, just dad and the neighbour to evade now and it was so easy that, although I was having fun, it was becoming a bit boring.

Finally I decided that it was time to call a halt but I needed to maintain my self respect, after all I did not want it to look as if I had been caught, a girl has her pride you know. The neighbour's car was parked adjacent to a derelict building, which was between the main road and the wood, and she was standing by the boot. She looked totally exhausted too. She called me sweetly so I pranced up to her ready to accept her fussing. As soon as I reached her I sat down and she grasped my collar.

"I've got her." She called.

"Oh brilliant." Panted dad from somewhere deep within the wood. Slowly he made his way over to us and clipped the lead on to my collar. This time he had the presence of mind to grab the lead from the hook behind the door before he gave chase.

Hello dad! Where were you?

I put on the most innocent expression I could manage as I looked up at him. We walked home but not before dad had heaped mountains of praise and thanks on the neighbour. I thought it great fun and I didn't even get told off.

The only other time I have escaped in Inglan was when mum and dad went to visit Dee, an old school friend of mum's, in Lewes. It was the first time I had visited her home so everything was new to me. I behaved myself impeccably all day, enjoyed a long walk through the local park with dad and explored the garden, which was four times the size of ours. Dad had taken my cage from the car and put it in their front room for three reasons. Firstly so that I would be able to sleep in a safe and secure place, secondly so that I would have a familiar place to go if I saw the need to be by myself, and thirdly in the highly unlikely event that I misbehaved it would be somewhere I could be banished to.

All went well on the first night, I had a good night sleep and awoke refreshed. When Dee got up early the following morning, she was always an early riser, she had let me out of the cage to stretch my legs, even though mum and dad were still in bed, while she fixed breakfast for Don, her husband. Don was the only person that had to go to work so after breakfast he donned, pardon the pun, his coat and opened the front door ready to leave. It was at this point that he suddenly realised that he had left his sandwiches in the fridge in the kitchen, he turned round and went to fetch them, leaving the front door wide open. What an opportunity, I did not need a second invitation. I ambled out of the front room, along the hallway and out through the open door. Don caught sight of my athletic rear quarters, as I strode confidently into the cold November air; he let out a despairing shout.

Too late Donald!

I know he didn't hear me but a smile of deep satisfaction spread across my face as I raced, like the very wind, up the road and away, intent on exploring the local area.

Their house backed onto thick mature woodland that fell down an incline to a large stream. On the other bank was a massive area of marshy meadowland which led up to the vast area known as the Sussex downs, so as you can appreciate, I had an infinite world to explore. And explore it I did, I went everywhere I could think of. Down the steep embankment I raced, through the trees that bordered the river, along the bank where I met a family of foxes, up through the trees again to a deserted allotment garden, across a very busy road. I explored everywhere.

In the beginning I heard mum, dad and Dee very faintly as they called my name in a futile attempt to convince me to return. No way, not until I am good and ready and that won't be for some time because I was on a mission. I totally ignored them. It didn't take long before their voices faded to nothing. I said 'hello' to the postman as I ran past him and called 'hi' to the bin men collecting the rubbish but apart from that I was on my own.

Mum, dad and Dee were the furthest thing from my mind at that point and I didn't realise that they were frantic with concern, partly for my safety and partly out of the fear that they might never see me again. Don was firmly in the doghouse and had been unceremoniously packed off to work because having recently suffered a hip replacement there was no way he could join in the search.

Mum walked around all of the estate roads searching for the merest sign of me, whilst dad, bless him, did a comprehensive search of the woodland, the riverbank and the allotment gardens. Obviously by the time he got to these places I had been and was long gone so as a result he saw neither hide nor hair of me. Mind you he did suffer rather.

Firstly he grabbed a low hanging branch as he inched his way down the woodland slope, which was quite steep for a human, only to find that the branch was rotten and it couldn't support his weight. It broke off with a crack and, losing his balance, he tumbled down the slope, hitting a couple of trees as he slid past and ended up in a thicket of brambles. He then slipped again as he approached the stream and fell, face first, into the stodgy mud, he rose looking more like Al Jolson than himself apparently. I wish I had been there to see that.

He eventually staggered back to Dee's house wet, muddy, scratched, bleeding and, for some strange reason, somewhat unhappy. Sorry dad, I didn't mean for anybody to get hurt.

Dee, for her part, walked down to the park where dad had taken me earlier and accosted all of the local dog walkers as they passed by her, recruiting them into the ever expanding search party. After that she went back to the house just in case I returned under my own volition.

Having exhausted all the places I could have been, and with dad cleaned up and in fresh clothes, mum and dad thought they could cover much more territory by car so they toured the area, quizzing the postman, the bin men and anybody else they encountered walking the streets either with or without a dog. Having had no luck they contacted the police, the local vet and the local dog patrol before going back to the house and sitting, somewhat dejectedly, to refresh themselves with a well earned coffee. I was fast becoming something of a local celebrity. They sipped their coffee and waited, what else could they do? Time marched on and they settled down to a sad lunch, even though they had no appetite, they were sick with worry because they had, by this time, convinced themselves that they had lost me for good, resigned to the fact that there was no way they would ever see me again. Dad opined sadly that even if I attempted to return to the house it was highly unlikely that I would be able to find my way back. Oh ye of little faith.

Happily I explored the local woods, fields and meadows for more than of four hours and enjoyed every single minute of the experience, but by midday I was beginning to feel a little hungry and thirsty, remember I had no breakfast, so I thought perhaps I had better make my way back to the house. My sense of direction was well honed from my lonely vigil on the mountains of Spain so I knew exactly where I was and where I had to go, mentally I plotted my return route and set off.

Fifteen minutes later I sauntered confidently down the road to Dee's house, turned into the driveway, walked up to the front door, sat down and barked once. You will remember that has always been my way of asking either to go in or to go out, one bark. Within seconds the front door was thrown open and I strolled in as if I owned the place, past an astounded dad, with a nonchalant expression on my face.

OK guys, so what's for lunch?

Their faces were a picture to behold, a mixture of relief, disbelief and incredulity. Unnecessarily they all made a big fuss of me, hugging me and kissing my snout, but I really didn't know what all the fuss was about. Of course I only found out about all their fun and games later as I listened to them reminiscing and later when they explained to Don what havoc he had unwittingly created. I did feel a little bit sorry for them; just a little bit. I was also a smidgen disappointed at their lack of confidence in me and my abilities. I had known at all times where I was and where the house was, I only popped out to explore the surrounding area and I always intended to come back when I was ready. Had I ever failed to return before? No, so why would I start now? Why would I even consider exchanging my new comfortable existence for a life on the run, I ask you. Humans, I swear I will never fully understand them.

Of course I have gone walk about on many occasions in Spain but mum and dad don't seem to be too bothered there. I guess it is partly because they know that I am totally familiar with my mountain and partly because there are no roads with busy traffic so I am completely safe.

The only time that they have been worried, and in all honesty I was rather worried too, was when a neighbour called to see them and left the gate open, not realising that I was loose on the terrace. I made my escape, skipping past him, up the steps to the track and away for a day of fun and rabbit chasing.

My usual routine in these instances is to run all over my territory for two or three hours, chase and catch the odd rabbit, just to keep my hand in you understand, and run past the house at intervals so that mum and dad will know that I am about. When I have had my fill of freedom for the day, when I am hot and tired or when I am hungry, I swagger down the steps and through the gate, which they always leave conveniently open for me, sit by the door and deliver my calling card, one bark.

This particular time, unbeknown to me, dad had to take his car to the local garage for a service, so half way through the morning it disappeared. Each time that I ran past the house I saw there was no car and assumed that they were not at home and as the day turned to evening and evening into night, with still no sign of car or habitation, I began to worry. Could it be possible that they had, by any chance, gone off to Inglan without me? I had caused them panic in the past, especially in Lewes, and now it was my turn to hit the panic button. I did the only thing I could do, I ran up the hill to visit Samson, I knew that I would always get a warm welcome there. Les was sitting on the terrace, enjoying the peaceful evening, sipping a gin and tonic when I ran onto the terrace.

"Hello Popps, what are you doing here? You shouldn't be out should you sweetheart?"

Mum and dad have abandoned me and gone away!

Les took me into the house and I lie down with Samson on his favourite sheepskin rug. He gave me an old fashioned look.

"What's all the fuss about Popp? You know there is no way on earth that your mum and dad would abandon you." Of course I knew he was right.

"Well where are they then? They have been out all day and now all night."

"I'm sure there is a logical explanation. Just relax girl."

Les telephoned dad who walked up with a lead to collect me. As I walked back past the empty parking space I thought to myself 'plonker Poppy'.

I had been running free for over ten hours that day and for once I frightened myself more than I frightened mum and dad.

I was now fast approaching my second birthday and I was getting used to living for long periods in Inglan. Dad had taken early retirement many years previously so he was able to be at home with me most days but mum still had her job as a doctor's receptionist, although she was by now considering retirement.

Life settled down into more of a natural routine, dad and I went walking each morning and during the afternoons I occupied the garden patio in a horizontal position, if the weather was not too cold, whilst dad did some housework, cooking, 'do it yourself' or some of his writing. If the weather was too cool to relax outside I would lie on the warm carpeted floor or even the sofa.

One of the excursions that dad and I used to make while mum was at work, that I really enjoyed, was when we went to visit dad's mother and father, nana and granddad to me. I must admit that I didn't take much to nana, she was a strange person, always miserable and forever talking about herself or saying nasty, hurtful things about other people. Worst was the way she used to order granddad about, constantly moaning at him.

As for Granddad, he was a completely different proposition. He was more than ninety years old and always smiling. Sadly he was already travelling down the Alzheimer's slope, so unfortunately I never got to know him when he was at his sharpest, and he also had a cancer growing in his neck that I detected the first time that I saw him. He loved me and I love him. It was wonderful to be with him. As soon as we arrived he would call me over to him so that he could rub my ears and generally fuss me.

We would go through to the sitting room of their little bungalow and he would sit in his armchair, constantly stroking my back and rubbing my ears. I lapped it up, two or three hours of constant fuss.

Best of all was when mum slipped him a handful of my soft chews, thinking that I hadn't seen the exchange, I played along and pretended not to have noticed. Granddad always broke the chews into four bite sized pieces and placed one of them on his knee, waiting for me to find it. I pretended to take a while to find it before offering to shake paws with him, we would shake and then he let me take the chew and eat it.

He would repeat the game with another piece of chew in his slipper, then one in his belt, one under his hand and so many more places. What he wanted was for me to sniff each of them out, ask for them, and then take them off him. This game would end when he held the last few pieces above his head, out of my reach but not out of my vision, until I had offered my paw. A simple game but we both loved it. I loved my granddad, I loved our visits to see him and I was very sad when they were brought to an abrupt end. Nana decided that I was persona non grata and told dad that I was no longer welcome in her house. Later, in February 2014, dad told me that granddad had died. I already knew, us dogs know these things, and it made me very sad.

Mum, dad and I would drive to Spain whenever we could, which means whenever mum could get time off work, and then I would be in my element. While we were away from Inglan mum had a friendly neighbour who fed and looked after the cats, and another friend who looked after the house. I loved my trips back to my Spanish home and always knew, as soon as we turned off the motorway and headed away from the Mediterranean, that I was back on my mountain once more.

Sadly, during one of these trips, we lost Pippa. She was a pretty tabby cat who always lived outside, she kept herself to herself so I didn't know her that well, but apparently one day she just didn't turn up for her food and was never seen again. Whether she became ill and hid up somewhere to die or whether somebody took a liking to her and stole her, we will never know. Mum was very upset.

I had now become a permanent fixture within the family and I felt a growing confidence as a direct result of that situation, so much so that I could begin to assert myself. There was one anomaly within the family that I was determined to resolve, that was the sleeping arrangements. I was not happy with the situation whereby I would have to spend the night sleeping on the sofa in the sitting room, even though I was covered with a soft warm blanket, while mum, dad, Simba and Ollie all slept upstairs. It was high time that I did something about it, so I formulated yet another plan.

I put phase one into operation after we all settled down to sleep one night. I waited until the early hours when I could hear gentle rhythmic snoring coming from upstairs, telling me that everybody was asleep, before delivering one of my doorbell barks. I didn't do it too loud, just enough to wake them. I knew mum and dad would have been asleep for a while and that would put them on the back foot right away. As expected they simply turned over and tried to return to dreamland, so I waited about a quarter of an hour and did it again, it was just enough to be annoying and must have been infuriating for them. I didn't have to do this many times before, as planned, dad called down to me to be quiet.

Not in the plan I'm afraid dad.

I persisted and dad responded sleepily until eventually he decided he had better come downstairs to see what my problem was. Naturally his first thought was that I wanted to go out for a pee so he walked across the living room, tired eyes like slits, opened the back door and waited for me to do my business, which I duly did. I wandered around the garden, had a leisurely pee, wandered back in and demanded fuss by rubbing my snout against his leg. Eventually I allowed myself to be settled on the sofa again.

The next night I repeated the process, and the next, only I didn't bother to go for a pee, I just let dad know that I wanted him to come downstairs. I simply wanted to be fussed, at three thirty in the morning!

I kept this up for three or four nights, dad was really resilient but the sleep deprivation was getting to him by now. He discussed it with mum and they decided that it might be a good idea to move me up into the bedroom and let me sleep there, at least that way they might get a full night's sleep again. They bought me a nice new basket, just like the one I had in our mountain home and placed it on the floor on dad's side of the bed.

Result! Thanks dad but it took a while for you to cotton on didn't it.

Seriously I believe I can get dad to do almost anything.

I let things settle for two or three weeks, mainly to lull mum and dad into a false sense of security, before I put phase two into operation. Once again I chose the early hours of the morning, when both mum and dad were snoring contentedly, before I made my next move. Very gently, so as not to wake either of them, I climbed onto the bed and curled up at the bottom by their feet and slept the sleep of the innocent. Invariably one of them would wake up later and realise that they could not move their legs which would prompt dad to assist me off the bed and back into my basket. Fine, I had included that in my contingency plan. It was always dad who would lift me from the bed because mum could never manage to lift me, mind you dad found it difficult enough. Have you ever tried to move twenty five kilogrammes of dog that didn't want to be moved and had become a dead weight? Well I can tell you that it is exhausting at the least and downright impossible at the worst. It only took a couple of days for dad to surrender and I had succeeded in becoming a permanent fixture at the foot of the bed.

This really is too easy!

A completed plan, you might think, but no I wasn't done yet. You see, often when mum was sound asleep, Ollie would jump onto the bed and curl up on her pillow, round her head, making her look, for all the world, like Davey Crockett. I had no aspirations to curl round anyone's head, that would be silly I'm much too big but I did want to be a bit more like them, so phase three saw me slowly creep up the bed so that I was between mum and dad, with my head near the pillow and my front paws on dad's chest. Now I had succeeded in bringing my plan to a satisfactory conclusion. Since then I begin every night curled up at the foot of their bed and end the night wherever I wish.

I have now progressed beyond my original plan and at bedtime, when I lie at the foot of the bed, I receive five delicious biscuits by way of a nightcap.

"She's the most effective contraceptive I've ever known." is the way dad often describes me and my sleeping antics. I don't pretend to understand exactly what he means by that, but I do take it as a compliment.

In November 2011, when I was about two and a half, mum decided to finally retire from work and she and dad planned to spend considerably more time in Spain. Unfortunately, the best laid plans of dogs and men and all that, fate had other ideas and aimed a big stick toward the spokes of their bike and steered life in a totally different direction.

Mum noticed that she was becoming less able to get around as she had been used to doing, for instance when climbing the stairs she found that she had to rest half way. She was almost permanently tired and it was simply explained away as a symptom of getting older. Even her doctor told her to eat less and exercise more and she would be ok. The crunch came when mum and dad had been to visit a friend who lived in the next road. It was February and there was some ice and snow around but the footpaths were mostly clear. As they made their way home on the three hundred metre walk mum had to stop to catch her breath three times. Dad said that enough was enough, something was definitely wrong and he wanted mum to see her doctor again.

Fortunately mum was unable to see her normal doctor and she saw a locum instead. The doctor was concerned and telephoned the hospital for mum to go there immediately. After a number of hospital visits involving x-rays, scans, blood tests, ECG's in fact the whole gambit, mum was eventually diagnosed with a serious heart condition. All plans for a quick return to Spain were put on hold until, following many more hospital visits and procedures, including having her heart stopped and restarted, mum was pronounced fit and given the all clear to resume a near normal life. I say near normal because she has to take twelve different tablets every day and she will have to keep taking them for the rest of her life.

We canines are extremely sensitive to human ailments and I had sensed some weeks before the problem came to a head that all was not well. I tried to give some indication but was lost for a way to persuade mum to consult her doctor. I cuddled up with her on the sofa most nights, and if she rested in bed during the day I would lie with her. I continued cuddling up and giving comfort until I knew that she was well on the mend, but, of course, I didn't stop there. I still cuddle up to her on the sofa or during the day on the bed but I have share myself and curl up with dad when we all watch the television, just to make sure that he doesn't get jealous.

With mum fighting fit again, well more like getting herself back to fitness, you would have thought that we could now return to Spain. Sadly this was still not to be the case, not yet anyway, you see 2012 was going to be a landmark year, a year of great change. Mum and dad had decided to get married and they duly tied the knot on the twenty fourth of June. I would love to tell you all about it, but unfortunately I can't, you see I was confined to boarding kennels for the duration and did not get to see any of it, nothing, zilch, nada.

Mind you the boarding kennels were really comfortable and I was treated like royalty. Up reasonably early in the morning the first item on the agenda was a nice long walk around the adjoining fields accompanied by an attractive young lady who kept fussing me. This was followed by breakfast and a bit of play time, again with the young lady, followed by a stimulating brush down, which made my coat shine like silk and a dash of talcum powder rubbed in to make me smell sweet. A complete pampering.

Late afternoon there was another walk followed by a few biscuits for supper and then relaxation in my very own exclusive pen. I could take this kennel treatment for ages, no sweat. I didn't want to go to this wedding thing anyway and it obviously wasn't anything to shout about because when I came home again everything was exactly the same, nothing had changed, big fuss about nothing if you ask me.

Shortly after the wedding we made the long overdue journey to our mountain home in Spain but this time we stayed for just over three months, and we took Ollie and Simba with us too. Dad's car, a Land Rover Freelander, was not that big inside, and with all the things that mum and dad wanted to take with them, space was at a premium so Ollie ended up sharing my cage with me, while Simba had her exclusive, if small, cage. I was quite happy to share with Ollie, that was fine with me, after all we were the best of friends and we often lie together on the sofa.

Simba just lie statuesque for the entire journey with her front paws tucked under her body and an unhappy expression on her face. Although I had my usual exercise breaks Ollie and Simba stoically refused to budge. Mum and dad had bought them each a special lead similar to mine but they made it almost impossible to put them on and then when lifted to the ground they refused to take even one step. Ultimately mum and dad left them in the cages in the car.

Once back in our mountain home we had a fantastic time, Sundays we would walk the entire length of the Paseo Maritimo, that's the seafront promenade in Torre del Mar. Dad was always armed with a pocketful of plastic nappy bags so that he could clean up after me if I had an 'accident' on the pavement. I always did but it was no accident, after all his efforts it would be a shame for him not to get to use them, wouldn't it. Some evenings mum and dad went for meals with friends and I was able to have a little time to myself, policing the terrace, guarding the home, while they were gone 'to the shops'.

I guess it was because neither mum nor dad had work to worry about that we spent far more time in Spain and less in Inglan after the wedding. Dad fitted a wood burning stove in the lounge which he fired up each night in the winter, making the whole house warm and cosy. I could lie in front of it until my coat began to singe.

Mum and dad eventually decided to spend at least eight months of the year on my mountain and little did I know, when we arrived in May the following year for our summer stint, that my life would, once more, change forever. I am so pleased it did because this was definitely a change for the better.

It all began rather innocuously when mum and dad visited friends of theirs who lived on the next mountain, they hadn't seen each other since we left in March so I was not surprised that they were gone for quite some time, when they finally arrived home they were deep in conversation.

"Isn't she beautiful, and so sweet." Dad was obviously taken by something, or someone.

"She is absolutely gorgeous." Mum agreed.

Excuse me! Who is this you are talking about?

I walked up to dad, looked him in the eye and tilted my head to one side, that usually got a reaction.

"And how she just lie on the sofa, so timid."

She! Who dad?

I tilted my head the other way. Still no reaction.

Hello! Here I am. Who is this 'she' dad.

"I would love to adopt her. What do you think?"

"I suppose two is just as easy as one, there is not much difference really. If that's what you want."

Two now! What is going on?

It seemed as if mum was in favour of whatever or whoever or how many this 'she' was. Dad, however, was still resisting my telepathy, time to try something else. I sat, looked dad squarely in the eyes and offered my paw. If that didn't work nothing would.

"What do you think Popps?"

What do I think of what, you haven't told me anything yet. Come on dad give me a break.

"You'll never guess Popps."

Of course I won't. GET ON WITH IT!

Then at last he let me into the big secret. Alan and Jan, their friends on the next mountain, often provided a foster home for a local animal charity, they would provide a temporary home for dogs or cats that had been abandoned or mistreated or both.

This time they were looking after a six month old puppy called Honey. She had been thrown out on the street in a village not too far away at the tender age of three months and had to survive by eating scraps and rummaging in rubbish. She had also been mistreated by the villagers who had thrown stones at her to frighten her off.

I was speechless. I knew exactly how she felt. Memories flooded back into my mind of the days immediately after I had escaped from the hunter. I too had raided rubbish bins. I had been pelted with stones by unfeeling humans. I had been there but I had been much older. I wondered if it was the same village that I had been so heartlessly expelled from. Maybe her mother had been one of the pack that I left behind when I quit the village. My heart went out to her, I desperately wanted to meet her.

Get her dad. Get Honey, I'll look after her.

Mum and dad made arrangements for me to meet Honey at the home of Alan and Jan, they thought it best for our first meeting to be on her home territory as it might make her feel more confident and less threatened. Then if for some unfathomable reason we did not get on we could be separated immediately, it seemed like a good idea to me.

A couple of days later we all piled into the car and turned up at their front door, I was excited to meet this poor pup. Dad kept me on my lead so that I would not be overpowering, I ask you do they think I'm stupid?

The first time I set eyes on her Honey was lying on the terrace looking extremely shy, slowly I walked over to her and gently sniffed her nether regions observing the correct protocol when you first meet. She recoiled, she was frightened of me. That was understandable in the circumstances but she had no reason to be. She shrank back and crawled backwards under a chair, all the time keeping me firmly in her gaze. Her tail was down, not between her legs because she had this lovely stumpy tail that would not curl between her legs no matter how she tried. Her ears were plastered to her head, she was displaying all of the outward signs of fear and uncertainty.

"This is Honey, Poppy, isn't she gorgeous?"

Let me handle this dad.

For once he seemed to hear me and sat himself down on a white plastic chair beside the table that Alan was busy covering with drinks and nibbles. I sat beside him. Fortunately for me, as soon as Alan began pouring the drinks an instant conversation started up between all four humans.

Good boy Alan, just the job.

With the humans engrossed in what was important to them I could concentrate on really getting Honey relaxed and begin the process of getting to know her; my way.

Dad had been right, she was a beautiful dog, light brown in colour, hence her name I guessed, with a darker brown round her eyes and snout, which made her look as if she were wearing a robber's mask, her eyes were like big brown pools a hundred metres deep. She was still cowering under the chair that Alan was sitting in, unsure of me, it would not take me long to change that.

"It's alright Honey, you needn't be afraid." I whispered. There was a brief twitch of her ears, she had heard me. She turned those beautiful eyes toward me and showed the whites to me. This was a sign designed to convey to me that she was still frightened but was feeling less threatened.

"My name is Poppy, I want to be your friend, I think that we can be very good friends; don't you."

"I don't know." That was a good start, she was talking to me, the bond could now be built on if I proceeded carefully.

"You've been hurt in the past haven't you." Her eyes turned to the floor. "I understand."

"Do you?"

"More than you know. I was treated badly by my first human. I was treated so badly that I ran away. I had to live by raiding rubbish bins and catching rabbits."

"What are rabbits?"

"That's a subject for later, for now you need love and companionship from somebody who knows what you went through." I paused to let it sink in, it was a lot for her to take in over so short a time. I told her an abbreviated version of my story, leaving out anything that she need not know yet, she listened intently.

"Would you like to tell me what happened to you? If you get it off your chest you will feel much better. There's no rush you can take all the time you need."

"What about the humans?" I looked up at dad, then mum, then Alan and Jan, they were all still deep in conversation oblivious to us. They had received our good vibrations, even if they were not aware of it.

"Oh don't worry about them, they have their drinks now and they can't hear us. So long as we appear to be quiet they will assume that all is well."

With that she told me her story which had distinct similarities to mine. She spoke slowly and there were some lengthy pauses, I didn't break the pauses I let her progress at her own speed, it was important for her to feel comfortable and unhurried.

She had been born under some old pieces of furniture on the terrace of an old house in a village, she didn't know which village or where it was. Her mother had either been given or had stolen a tattered and torn blanket which provided the only comfort they had. There had been five puppies in all, she had two brothers and two sisters. The family had stayed together with her mother until they were three months old and then the humans had taken one of the sisters away, mother said that she was destined for a hunter friend of the human, to breed from. A shiver ran down my spine, I understood only too well the horrific life the sister had been cast into.

Having no use for the remaining puppies, and with nobody to give them to, they had all been cast out onto the street to fend for themselves. One sister and one brother had disappeared in the first couple of days and she never saw them again, but one of her brothers and one of her sisters remained with her.

Together they scavenged for food, constantly being chased off and stoned by children and adults alike, until one day some children from the village set upon them with sticks and large stones. Her sister ran away, Honey never even noticed in which direction she went, but her brother tried to protect her, he stood in front of her barking fiercely at the children whilst telling her to run. She ran, but not far, she watched from a safe distance, desperately wanting to go back and help but knowing it would be more difficult for him if she did. She looked on in horror as one heavily built boy lashed at her brother with a thick stick, her brother yelped with the pain, the thug kicked him hard in the underside. She could stand it no longer and dived in to help her injured brother, then the thugs turned on her too. She didn't know what to do.

When it seemed that nothing could stop the onslaught a passing car screeched to a halt, the occupants, a middle aged couple, jumped out and shouted for the children to stop. The stick wielding rabble melted into the landscape like water on a tablecloth. Honey's brother was on his side whimpering with the pain. The couple scooped him up, collected a terrified Honey, and placed them both on the rear seat of their car.

Honey looked out of the rear window as the car pulled away, the children reappeared, their bravado returning now that the car and its furious occupants were disappearing, they seemed somehow disappointed that their sport was disappearing too. Of their sister there was no sign.

Honey and her brother were taken to a vetinerary practice in Velez Málaga where they were checked over. Honey had only superficial bruises but was severely shaken and extremely frightened. She shook with fear as she was examined despite the comforting efforts of the nurse. Turning her head to look at her brother she saw that he was lying on his side, the vet bent over him with a worried look on her face.

"He is in a bad way." She said shaking her head, angry at the way he had been beaten. "He has a broken leg, three broken ribs, lots of bruising to the abdomen and a number of cuts." The couple who had saved them both had tears in their eyes. "Of course I don't know what internal damage there is but if it is only bruising he will be alright, given time and a loving environment." She added.

That night Honey had stayed in a cage at the vet with her brother in the cage beside her. He was bandaged, plastered and sedated with a bottle fixed to the cage dripping remedial medicine through a needle attached to his front leg, just above his paw.

The next morning a kindly lady from a local animal rescue charity called to take Honey to her new temporary foster home. As she walked tentatively out of the door she turned once more to gaze upon her brave brother who had undoubtedly saved her life. He was still sedated. The drip continued rhythmically. It was to be the last time she saw him.

Two days later and Honey was with Alan and Jan being pampered and fussed, she didn't respond initially, her thoughts were firmly fixed on her brother but she perked up considerably the following week when the lady from the rescue charity called to see how she was progressing. Honey wanted to know about her brother but how could she ask?

"How is her brother getting along?" Jan wanted to know.

Thanks Jan for asking for me.

Honey's ears pricked, desperate for the answer but at the same time dreading it.

"Oh he's doing very well." Said the lady with a bright smile on her face. "The vet says there was no internal damage and he is mending nicely. He should be able to go to a foster home of his own in another week." She paused. "I don't suppose...."

"No I'm sorry." Jan knew what was coming and it hurt her to give the answer that she knew she must. "We would love to but with three cats as well as Honey, there just isn't room for any more."

Inside Honey was so happy, her brave brother would be alright, but her happiness was tinged with sadness that he would not be joining her. She had curled up on the sofa and slept soundly.

When she finished telling me her story I wanted to cry, she had been through so much worse than me. Slowly I stood up, stretched nonchalantly, and slowly made my way over to her. The humans were oblivious, they had their own conversations going. I licked her ear and whispered softly.

"You will be fine now, I know mum and dad want you to live with us. You and I can be together forever. If that is what you would like." Honey smiled, I went back to lie beside dad, winked at her and smiled. I realised then that I loved Honey as if she were my sister.

Me and dad over the meadows

My muddy bum, and I missed the squirrel.

My mate Ollie, I loved him so much.

Handsome Samson, my boyfriend.

Honey, my sister. We are inseparable.

Dozing in front of the television, together as always.

Rosita joined the family in 2013.

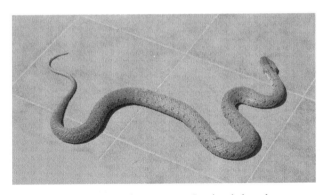

An unwanted guest on the terrace. I raised the alarm.

Jasper joined the family in 2015.

Honey treats Jasper as her baby.

The arrangements were made that in two days we would go and collect Honey from Alan and Jan. You are probably wondering why the delay, apparently another couple had registered an interest in adopting Honey and the rescue charity had to make their decision as to where she went. Jan made sure that the charity was aware of the deep bond that had been established between us and that mum and dad were experienced parents to their furry friends.

Thankfully the charity approved the adoption immediately, I had a sister.

Whooo hoo!

It was a Saturday morning and I was so excited, Honey was due to arrive the next day and stay forever. I lie on the terrace deep in thought, in my mind we were already playing together, eating together and talking girly nonsense. I was rudely awakened from my reverie as the phone rang, dad answered.

"Oh no!" he said in a worried tone.

What's up dad?

"Oh no!"

Dad you're worrying me now.

"Don't worry we will be right over."

What's happened?

"What's happened?" Mum asked.

I just said that mum.

"Alan was going to take Honey for a walk, he dropped his walking stick and it hit the door reja making a loud bang."

Hardly a topic for the front page of 'The Sun', I thought it was something important.

"It spooked Honey and she pulled the lead out of Alan's hand. She's run off."

I don't know, maybe it is a big deal after all.

I was concerned to hear the rest of the story.

"They have been searching for her for an hour or more without a sign. She has disappeared. Jan is frantic, she is in tears."

Oh no!

Dad had said that, could it be the start of reverse telepathy; nah!

"Oh no!" Mum joined in the chorus.

"I said that we would go right over and help them look for her."

"Too right." Mum was keen to get started. "I'll get my trainers on, I'll be ready in two minutes."

Take me too dad, please, take me too.

"You had better come too Popps, I'll get your lead."

Yes!

Telepathy rules.

Dad quickly drove us up to Alan and Jan's house and together they organised a search pattern. Apparently their biggest concern was the lead, which was still attached to her collar, it was an extending type similar to mine and the catch was off so it could have extended to five metres long, which meant that it could easily get tangled around a bush or tree trapping her where nobody could see her, she might even strangle herself in her struggle to be free.

There were four directions that Honey could have taken in her panic, assuming that she kept to the tracks. Alan had watched her run up the mountain so we could discount one of them, three tracks to search. It was decided that we would search along the tracks first and if we had no luck we would begin another search away from the tracks. That would be more difficult and would mean quartering the landscape, I hoped to goodness that she had the sense to keep to the tracks. Of the three tracks, one led down the left hand side of the mountain, another led down the right hand side and the final one carried on along the top of the ridge.

I know which way she went dad. I can follow her scent. Take the track along the ridge.

"Chris, you go down the track to the left, that's an easier route with your heart problem." My dad thinks of everything.

She went along the ridge dad!

"Alan you take the track to the right, Poppy and I will go along the ridge."

Yay! We got the ridge. Good boy dad.

"Jan you stay at the house in case she comes back on her own." My dad is a good organiser.

Off we all set. The humans called out to each other at regular intervals until they were finally out of each other's earshot.

They were all calling Honey's name, hoping against hope that she would hear them and come to heel but I knew that would not happen, she was frightened, she would hide up somewhere and wait to be discovered.

Dad and I had gone about a mile with no sign, I was confident that we were going in the right direction. I had her scent, I just hoped that it was not wishful thinking on my part. I stopped dead in my tracks. The scent had vanished.

"What's up Popps?"

Quiet dad, I'm searching for her scent and listening for any give away sound.

I heard a barely audible sound. There it was again, a faint sobbing. I knew dad could not hear it and I also recognised that it was unmistakably Honey. We walked a little further along the track, but more slowly now, the cry became louder. The track was in a kind of cutting, with the brush covered sides rising up to human waist level and then dropping away sharply on the other side of the rise. It was impossible to see over the top, even for dad, but I reached a point where I was confident we were close to her.

I climbed up the side of the rise and my nose caught her scent again, she had left the track and climbed over the side. I followed the scent down the slope on the other side. There beneath an almond tree, cowering under the undergrowth lie Honey. She was crying, unable to move, her lead wound tightly round the spindly trunk. Dad followed me over the crest and by the time he slithered down the slope I was lying beside Honey, dad thought I was licking her ears but in reality I was talking to her, reassuring her.

"We found her." Dad shouted as loudly as he could. There was no reply, we were still out of earshot of the other searchers.

He untangled Honey's lead and set her free, she licked him, I could see his heart melt. He turned to me.

"You are amazing poppy, you went straight to her, how did you know where she was?"

Elementary my dear dad I used my nose!

He made a terrific fuss of me, rubbing my ears, my chest and my tummy before kissing my snout.

Leave it out dad!

"C'mon girls, let's go home."

As we made our way back to Jan's house Honey and I walked really close, our flanks rubbing against one another in a gesture of love.

"Thanks Popps."

"Don't mention it Hun."

We sauntered along the track, retracing our steps, dad all the time calling out to mum and Alan, eventually there came a reply.

"What? Have you found her?" It was mum.

"No I haven't but Poppy has, we're bringing her home." A few more shouts and Alan also heard the good news, Honey was safe.

We arrived back at Alan and Jan's house in victory, everybody thought I had done an exceptional job in finding Honey. They all made a big fuss of us both and when dad related exactly how I had located Honey they all agreed that I was one very intelligent girl.

Was there ever any doubt.

The kettle went on so that the humans could have a nice hot cup of tea whilst Honey and I had a bowl of water, great is that it? Then we were rewarded with a couple of biscuits. Mind you Honey kept so close to me we could have been in the same skin. She leaned against me and rubbed the side of her head on my neck. I liked that.

Alan and Jan agreed that it would be unkind to separate us, now that we were obviously very close to each other, and agreed that she should come home with us immediately so that she could become settled.

It was the first time that Honey had been to our home so I decided to introduce her to Ollie and Simba, then she could find a nice quiet corner to settle into until she was ready for more. Ollie was his usual friendly self and he took to Honey straight away, they touched noses within five minutes, that is the accepted sign of welcome between a cat and a dog. Not so with Simba, she just harrumphed and headed toward her furry bed in the third bedroom muttering about another dog in her house.

"Don't mind her." Ollie told Honey. "It's nothing personal, she's like that with everybody."

That evening mum and dad were sitting on the terrace with a glass of wine, watching the reddening sun as it slipped slowly to kiss the mountains with the brilliant red glow of a typical Andalucian sunset. Dad suddenly looked pensive, he put his glass on the coffee table.

"You realise that with two dogs and two cats we will have to change the car don't you? There's no way we are going to get that lot in the one we have now." Mum looked over the rim of her glass.

"I suppose so."

"Mind you the old Land Rover is ten years old and getting a bit past it, so I suppose it's about time."

"What will we get?"

"Haven't got a clue yet, but it will have to be fairly big to get this lot in together with anything else we want to ship over."

Conveniently, the next morning, they had to go with Jan to the vet, a different one to the one I saw, in order to get the ownership document for Honey transferred from the charity to Dad, and they took advantage of this trip to look at some new motors. I went along for the ride, I was not about to be separated from Honey. I think that dad had decided on the kind of vehicle he wanted, just a matter of deciding what make and where he would find one. As we passed a car sale yard dad suddenly looked excited.

"That's the sort of car we need." He exclaimed, and with that he went all the way round a roundabout and headed back to the garage. He had spotted what he was after, a six-seater van with room behind the rear seats for two large and two small cages, plus loads of other stuff.

Another week and the new motor stood proudly on the driveway and two days after that dad had built a wooden table that slid into the space behind the rear seats so that our cages would be elevated to window level and we would be able to see where we were going, or more accurately where we had come from. After the conversion Dad never called it a van any more, he jokingly called it a 'specially modified estate management vehicle'.

Wally.

All that was left to do now was for Honey to have her final vaccinations and be issued with her passport, without which she would not be coming back to Inglan with us.

I went along, to provide her with moral support, just to reassure her you understand. The four of us trooped through the door and were greeted by the ever smiling Rosie, Carolina's receptionist, who jumped up and came round the counter to see mum.

"It's a very good thing that you came today." She beamed. "We have a special offer, for every consultation we are giving away a free kitten." With that she bent down to open a cage, which stood on the floor, took a tiny kitten out and placed it on mum's chest. It was obvious that mum loved it but reluctantly she handed it back to Rosie.

"We can't have it Rosie." She explained. "We have only just adopted Honey, and that was unexpected, we have two cats and two dogs now."

That seemed to be that, Carolina called us into the consulting room and Honey had her jabs. Job done then. Don't you believe it, when we returned to the reception area Rosie was still there with the little kitten. She explained that a kindle of kittens had been dumped in a rubbish bin and they would have died if a passerby had not heard them mewing and rescued them. The kindle was taken to Carolina so that new homes could be found for them. Unfortunately one kitten, the one that mum was now cuddling, had been very ill and nearly died. Carolina had treated her for ten days and she was now well enough to be re-homed. The remaining kittens had already gone to new homes. Mum looked at dad, even I recognised that look. Dad smiled at her.

"Well sweetheart, I just adopted Honey so I can't really complain if you want to adopt this little one can I."

You two are real softies when it comes to animals.

And the rest, as they say, is history. Mum and dad left with a new kitten that they christened Rosita, after the receptionist who had persuaded mum to adopt her, not that she needed much persuasion.

We were now five.

Good job you got that van dad. Erm, I mean 'specially modified estate management vehicle' of course.

The summer of 2013 was an idyllic time, the sun shone, I had a new sister that I loved dearly and she felt the same way about me. We had our three feline brother and sisters. Simba kept herself to herself but, following the removal of four decayed teeth which had obviously been giving her considerable pain and discomfort, she mellowed. Ollie was his usual laid back self, passing his time sleeping under his favourite jasmine bush, climbing on the roof of the study or stretching out on the sun lounger when he had enough of exercise for the day.

Rosita, being young, was a bit of a pest at times but on the whole she gave us no trouble. In the early days she had to spend most of her time on the terrace in Honey's wire cage until she had all of her vaccinations. Even then mum and dad kept her incarcerated until she grew a bit bigger. The problem was that if she roamed the mountain at that tender age she might get lost, be attacked by the wild dogs that occasionally roamed the mountain, or worse, being of slight build, she was at risk of being plucked up by one of the short clawed eagles or vultures that circled the mountain at intervals.

Mum was happy because she had her four legged family and dad was happy because he had a new vehicle to polish.

All too soon the summer came to an end and mum and dad made plans for our holiday in Inglan. Not only that but they were also planning to go to Florida which is in a place called Merica apparently. The drive back to Inglan was uneventful except for the fact that after only an hour on the road Rosita decided to have a good moan before having a poo in her cage. It stank really foul, offending my sensitive nose. Dad had to stop and take her out of her travelling cage while mum cleaned up the mess and changed the newspaper. Then Rosita herself was cleaned up and we were able to get back on the road again. The smell lingered for some time in the car despite the air conditioning running full blast. That's the trouble with cats, their poo smells awful, not like us canines.

It was good to return to the walks over the green meadows, a first for Honey of course, and I reacquainted myself with the other dogs that I had befriended the last time.

"Who is this pretty girl with you?" was the question on all their lips.

"This is my new sister, Honey." I told them, she got as much fuss as me from the other dog walkers but her timidity returned. She needed constant reassurance from me for each new experience, she was, and still is, very wary of anything unfamiliar.

Dad told everybody that Honey was called a 'Podencador' which raised a few eyebrows until he explained that was because she was half Podenco, like me, and half Labrador, unlike me.

We did, however, have one frightening experience while we were walking over the meadows. We were passing through the belt of trees adjacent to the brook, not far from where I did my swan dive into the mud chasing a squirrel, when a Staffordshire Bull Terrier came loafing around the corner in front of us. He had no lead on and there was no owner in sight so he was out of control. Honey shrank back and I tensed myself, I could sense that dad was apprehensive.

I have heard that this breed of dog gets a bad press but all dog owners, no matter what breed you have, ought to appreciate that, given the right combination of circumstances any of us can turn vicious. This is especially true of these ugly, overweight, ignorant excuses for a dog, and the one we met proved my point. He stood stock still for a short while with his wide set bandy legs firmly planted in the firm dirt of the path.

Then without warning he ran directly at Honey, snarling and slobbering, Honey pressed herself into dad's leg for protection. Instinct told me that dad would be unable to tackle this raging lump, Honey too would be powerless because of her frightened nature, that left just me.

As the growling mass approached Honey, and dad's vulnerable leg, at speed, I crept behind dad and readied myself. I knew that if he were to get his jaws anywhere near any one of us it would be almost impossible to break his hold, therefore I had to make the first move and I had to get it right. When the Staffy was almost upon dad and Honey I rounded dad's leg and leapt as high in the air as I could, landing heavily in the centre of his back. He was taken completely by surprise, his legs splayed out causing his chest to hit the ground. He was only slightly winded but before he could regain his feet or his composure I clamped my jaws around his neck and gripped harder than I have ever gripped before.

He wriggled and yelped with the pain which only encouraged me to grip even harder. He told me that enough was enough and he yielded. I was not going to be fooled so I hung on. At that point his owner rounded the corner and took in the scene with an astonished look on his face. Not until his lead was firmly clipped to his collar did I release my grip. His owner pulled him to heel and we stared hard at each other.

"Keep your distance from my family in future." I warned him. He just glared at me.

Dad and the other owner exchanged a few words, dads were mainly of warning, the other owner's were largely of contrition and apology.

Nobody messes with my family, I may be lightweight but believe me I am a formidable opponent. Just ask that Staffy.

When the time came for mum and dad to go to this Merica place I hoped that we would go with them in the van, but I was to be disappointed. We were in fact destined for the kennel that I had holidayed in when they had their wedding, we being me, Honey and Rosita. It appears mum and dad had to go in a big 'plane' and animals are not allowed to go in them, never mind I always enjoy staying in that kennel because I really get spoilt. Rosita came with us because she was too young to be left in the house like Ollie and Simba, they had a friend called Karen who called in twice a day to feed them, let them out into the garden and change the poo tray. It's easy for cats because they sleep nearly all the time and don't need to be exercised.

Mum and dad were in Merica for just over two weeks. Their return triggered a shopping spree, which excited me because I knew what this meant, they were stocking up on food and other goodies in preparation for the long journey back to my mountain home.

Sure enough two weeks later dad squeezed everything they had purchased into the van, followed by us two dogs and three cats and away we sped. Dad had chosen not to use boat to cross the channel anymore because he said it took too long, it was uncomfortable and for some unfortunate reason we always seemed to catch a boat with hoards of schoolchildren running around all the time. We now used the tunnel which was more convenient and cheaper. As usual we crossed late at night so that dad could get in a couple of hours driving in France before stopping for a sleep.

We pets didn't really need one because we had slept almost continuously since we left our Inglan home, but we had one anyway. On the road again early the next morning we made good time and the journey went well. That is until we got half way down France, somewhere near Tours I think, when we had to stop for another clean up exercise for Rosita.

Dad parked the car in a roadside picnic area and dad lifted her cage out of the back of the car, placed it on a plastic cloth on the driver's seat, took Rosita out of the cage and cuddled her while mum cleaned the cage and renewed the newspaper. For no apparent reason the cage suddenly slipped off the seat and hit the tarmac with a loud crash. Rosita was spooked and she leapt out of dad's arms, onto the tarmac and away into the bushes despite his efforts to stop her.

"Oh my goodness, look at you." Mum exclaimed in a concerned voice. I turned to look at dad and saw the reason for her concern. In her eagerness to run off Rosita had run her claws down dad's arm tearing the skin so that blood ran freely down his forearm and dripped off his fingers to mingle with the dirt on the tarmac. Not only that but she had also clawed his upper lip and blood oozed from beneath a large flap of skin.

Rosita had to take second place while dad wrapped an old towel round his arm to stop the flow of blood and mum held another towel to his torn face. Fortunately for dad, the bleeding stopped fairly rapidly and their attention turned to the important task of finding Rosita. For half an hour they walked along the hedgerow, calling her name continually and poking under the bushes, all to no avail. They searched a picnic area near the parking place, the adjoining fields and once more under all the bushes near the car. Nothing. Not so much as a whisker.

I could sense that they were becoming very concerned and distraught.

"I think it best if we just lie here quietly Honey, they have enough on their plate at the moment."

"I agree. I hope that they find her though."

"I'm sure they will." I said with more conviction in my voice than I felt in my heart.

They had been searching for over an hour with no sign whatsoever, hearts were beginning to sink.

"We can't stay here indefinitely." Dad voiced what we were all thinking. "I'll make us a cup of coffee, see if she reappears. If she doesn't we will be forced to leave her behind."

"She won't survive, she's too young. If we leave we will be condemning her to death." Mum was in tears, I wanted to comfort her.

"I know; but what option do we have."

"You're right of course."

Dad made the coffee, the little electric kettle they plugged into the cigarette lighter too ages to boil, they both waited longer than necessary for it to cool down and then drank it more slowly than they normally did. It was understandable, they were dragging everything out to its extreme because they didn't want to leave her behind until they had explored every possible hiding place and given her every chance to reappear. With the coffee making paraphernalia stowed away they decided to make one final round of the hedgerows and bushes before being forced to call it a day, then reluctantly they would have to abandon her to her fate. Still there was no sign.

Painfully the decision was made to continue the journey without Rosita. The look of heartbreak on their faces told its own story.

Mum was climbing into the passenger seat when she stopped dead in her tracks.

"Did you hear that?"

"I didn't hear anything." Not surprising as dad's hearing is slightly impaired and he suffers from tinitis.

"I'm sure I heard Rosita."

"Come on then let's look again." Dad needed no persuasion. Mum stood by the hedgerow and called Rosita's name. Sure enough there was a faint mewing sound.

"She's definitely in there somewhere." Dad confirmed. "Call her again and see if we can narrow it down a bit." Mum called. Rosita replied.

"She's over to our right, call again." Another call, another reply. Dad narrowed the search area still further.

Another series of calls and more responding miaows and she was located, deep inside a thorn bush. As they peered into the bush a small, terrified little face, stared wide eyed right into mum's eyes. Mum kept a careful watch in case she should move, while dad retrieved her cage from the car. He held the cage firmly, with the door open, waiting.

It was no use dad trying to catch her because she had a habit of running away from him whereas she always enjoyed a cuddle with mum. Mum steeled herself before plunging her arm deep into the thorn bush and grabbing Rosita by the neck and tugging with all her might. Fortunately the safety collar did not break open and a bedraggled cat, covered in thorns and dried leaves was pulled roughly through the spiteful thorns and stuffed unceremoniously into her cage all in one swift action.

Dad wasted no time in securing the door. Against all the odds Rosita was safe.

Now it was mum's turn to have a multitude of scratches treated. I must say they looked a right pair smothered in antiseptic cream and beaming smiles, the relief was palpable.

Dad waited another quarter of an hour for everybody to regain their composure before resuming the journey. In the back, unnoticed, we all began the process of unwinding and de-stressing too. In total we had been stopped for almost two and a half hours. Not bad just to clean poo out of a cage. As we departed I turned to Rosita.

"Good to have you on board, you had us all worried there girl."

"You were worried? What about me, I was absolutely petrified."

"Welcome home." I winked.

2014 turned out to be a very warm and dry summer in Andalucia. Honey and I lazed around on the terrace, Ollie spent great chunks of time under his favourite Jasmine bush as usual, Simba stayed cool indoors and Rosita climbed the Almond trees or hunted geckos in the shrubs.

One hot sunny afternoon, I had my eyes and ears on shutdown but my powerful nose was on sentry duty. It might seem to the uninitiated that I lie on the terrace with my eyes and ears firmly closed and that I am oblivious to all around me, but those who really know me know only too well that I am ever vigilant. This day I needed to be.

A distinctive aroma drifted up my nostrils and hit my million or so smell sensors, instinctively I knew that danger was among us. Slowly I rose to my feet, lifted my snout and located the direction from which the aroma was originating. It was wafting over the balustrade at the end of the terrace. I crept toward the smell, knowing full well what was causing it, the pungent salty smell could only come from one source. Cautiously I looked over the balustrade wall and looked straight into a golden eye with a pupil as black as coal. It was set in a silvery green armoured head and a jet black tongue flicked its forked fingers at me smelling me to determine if I posed a threat.

I backed off a metre and gave my bark of alarm. This is similar to my doorbell bark only not as loud, more of a whine and a bark combined. My whinbark had been heard by dad many times and he knew exactly what I was saying, only thing was that every other time I had warned of a snake it had been for a Lataste's viper which is usually only thirty centimetres or so long and is frightened of humans. Having said that it is venomous, although not too bad for a human, giving nothing more than a severe bout of nausea, it can be fatal for a cat or small dog though. This one was different it was a Montpellier, not only that it was a big adult Montpellier. Its sleek, light green body was at least two metres long and although unlikely to attack a human it could easily attack a cat or kitten.

I gave a couple more whinbarks.

Where are you dad? If mum sees this she will have kittens of her very own.

Two more whinbarks.

Dad! Dad! Hurry up.

"What's up Popps?" At last dad decided to stir himself. His face was a picture when he set eyes on the sleek green tube slithering over the wall onto the terrace. He disappeared into the house, that's dad not the snake, no doubt to get his gun I thought.

"Keep off the terrace Chris." I heard him shout. "There's a big snake, I'll let you know when I have got rid of it." A few minutes later he emerged with his camera in his hand. I couldn't believe it, the first thing he wanted to do was take a few photographs of it.

Yes I bet he's terrified of you dad, threatening him with a lens no less. I'll get rid of him for you should I then?

I waited until its tail slapped onto the terrace before I began to harass it. I went for its tail and gave it a sharp nip. Hissing Sid turned toward me his cavernous mouth wide open and his sharp, scimitar shaped fangs ready to bite.

"Careful Poppy, don't annoy it."

What do you suggest I do dad, read it a bedtime story?

I turned my attention back to the gaping jaw.

"You don't frighten me sunshine." I assumed my most confident and authoritarian voice. Sid seemed to understand and began to slither away. I encouraged him to hurry up by nipping his tail again. His head whipped round with a loud hiss.

"Will you stop doing that, I'm going as fast as I can." He spat at me. His eyes glinted as he spied the entrance to a water spout and he began to wriggle toward it. He turned to me one last time and hissed.

"I'll be back."

"Yes alright Arnie now scram." Another nip and his head disappeared into the water spout. Two more nips and he slipped silently out of the gargoyle on the other side and flopped onto the garden border below. Without a pause he glided over the border wall landing on the pool terrace with a painful slap. I had raced down the steps to the pool area to make sure he didn't have a change of mind and stay. He gave me one last look before slithering under the gate, into the rough undergrowth and disappearing.

"Right where is he?" dad emerged from the house with his gun in his hand ready for business, he was busy slotting a lead pellet into the barrel and priming the air cylinder. "Where has he gone?"

You're too slow dad, I've dealt with him.

"Did you ..... you are a good girl Popps, you're a very brave girl. Chris, Popps chased him away, it's OK to come out now." He hadn't noticed that while he was shooting glamour photographs and fumbling for his gun mum had watched me as I dispatched the unwelcome visitor. Dad aimed his gun at a rock and squeezed the trigger. The pellet cracked against the stone. The gun was safe again now.

I walked slowly across to where I had been lying and stretched myself out again, closed my eyes and ears and smiled to myself. Dad is a wuss, but he's harmless.

The weeks slowly slipped away, once again everything seemed perfect. Everything was perfect. Only thing is, I have discovered over the years that it is often when things seem to be going smoothly that something rears up and bites your tail. It had happened when I found my ideal village, only to be attacked by the inhabitants. It happened again when Boy's dad abandoned me just when I thought I had a family again. Yet again it happened when mum finally retired and then developed acute heart failure.

Sadly in the spring we had lost granddad, he finally succumbed to his cancer and Alzheimers at the age of ninety three. I would never again be able to pretend to find the chews that he had hidden. Now misfortune was about to happen once more. It all started one day when Ollie began to act strangely, he went off all day on his own, only coming back home at bedtime which was most unusual, he was normally within sight most of the time. Over the next couple of days he hid himself away, he even stopped eating which was very worrying because he always loved his food. Mum picked him up and cuddled him as often as she could and the lines of worry started to creep across her face. Normally we animals get well all on our own if left alone for a few days, but this was not the case with Ollie, gradually he became worse.

"We should take him to the vet." The concern was clear in mum's voice.

"I agree." Said dad. "We will go right away." Ollie was gently lifted into his travelling cage and mum and dad climbed into the car and disappeared. I wanted to go with them, after all he was my mate, but I suppose I would have been in the way.

When they returned it was evident that they were still very concerned. Ollie had a very high temperature and the vet thought it might be an infection and had given him an antibiotic injection and another intended to perk up his appetite. He looked a bit better as he lie on the sun lounger on the terrace. He looked at me with sad painful eyes.

"How are you doing old mate?"

"Not so good Popps. I still don't feel like eating, in fact I don't feel like doing anything, I seem to have no energy at all. I've got this funny feeling in my tummy too."

I laid down beside him and licked his face. He gave me a resigned half smile and I knew. I knew what mum and dad had yet to discover, Ollie was not going to make it. I cried as I nuzzled him.

"I'm here old fella, I'll stay with you, keep you company."

"Thanks Popps."

The next morning Ollie was worse so mum and dad took him off to the vet again.

"I don't think I will be coming back Popps." He whispered as dad walked past me with his cage.

"Of course you will mate, keep your chin up. I'll see you later." In my heart I knew he was right.

Mum and dad came home without him, both visibly upset, Ollie was mum's favourite, as far as she had favourites, and that was fine with the rest of us, he was the figurehead amongst us pets: the gaffer. As mum and dad talked I picked up the details without encroaching on their discomfort. Honey, Simba and Rosita all behaved impeccably, giving mum and dad an easy time.

When Carolina had examined Ollie she was very concerned because his injections should have given him a boost, but there was no improvement, in fact there was further deterioration. She took a blood test and discovered that he had leukaemia, a sort of cancer of the blood or bone marrow. There was a treatment available that was extremely expensive but which, unfortunately, carried no guarantees. Where the four legged family was concerned money has never been an issue for mum and dad so they had asked Carolina to begin the treatment immediately, he had to be given the best chance possible.

Two days later they received the phone call they had been dreading. Ollie had passed away. Mum was distraught because she had not had the opportunity to say a proper goodbye to him because his decline had been so rapid toward the end.

I went outside, I wanted to be alone, I had lost my old mate. The only crumb of comfort was that he would not have to suffer any more. Again I cried.

That autumn only the six of us went back to Inglan, that's not strictly true, we carried Ollie's ashes back with us so you could say we were all still together one way or another.

Mum intended to bury Ollie's ashes where Sophie, his great soul mate, had been buried but when it came to it, understandably, she couldn't part with him, not yet anyway, so he stands proudly on the bookcase that he often used to lie on.

Somehow neither house seemed the same without Ollie, it was wrong for there to be only six of us in the car when we made the long journey back to Spain in the spring of 2015. It was an emptiness that was soon to be filled, and how.

Unlike Honey and me the cats are rather fussy about their food, whereas we will eat almost anything they often turn their collective noses up at something they ate happily the previous week. Fickle creatures, cats. The upshot of this is that mum always has little bits of uneaten cat food which she collects and keeps in the fridge until she has a large polystyrene tray full. When they go out, to the shops of course, mum places the tray of food behind the rubbish bins to give the stray cats something to eat. Odd times, in addition to the spare food, she would take some cat biscuits or even some of mine and Honey's biscuits, into the village and feed the stray cats and dogs there. As you have obviously noticed by now mum is a real softie when it comes to stray animals, and dad says that if she had her way they would end up with cats, dogs, goats, ponies and goodness knows what else, even a giraffe, but I don't know what one of them is so I can't comment.

Mum has a big heart, literally and there's nothing wrong with having a big heart is there.

So, it came to pass that one day when dad stopped off at the rubbish bins to dump the recycling, mum disappeared behind the bins laden with excess cat food and when she emerged she was not alone, in her arms she held the smallest kitten I had ever seen, smaller even than Rosita had been when she joined the family.

"Oh Dave, look what I have found. Isn't he gorgeous."

This tiny bundle of ginger and white fur lie in mum's arms looking up at her with great big soft blue eyes. Her heart melted.

Here we go again dad, I foresee a new family member.

"I think you are right Popps."

You heard me!

"He looks gorgeous Chris."

"We can't leave him here, there is no mother in sight and he is far too young to survive on his own and by the way he is gnawing at my finger he is pretty hungry too, I think he has either been abandoned or something has happened to his mother."

The shopping trip was duly abandoned as the car was turned around and the little bundle was taken home. Mum placed him in one of the travelling cages for safety and proceeded to prepare some easily digested food for him. He was ravenous and eagerly devoured any and everything that was placed in front of him, underlining mum's conviction that he had been abandoned.

"We must find a name for him, one that reflects him accurately." All the usual names for a ginger cat were trotted out but none of them struck the right chord. Ginger,

Marmalade, Marmaduke and Jaffa were all considered but found to be wanting so he went without a name for a couple of days. It wasn't until mum's good friend Shirley came round that he was finally christened.

"What about Jasper, for Jasper Carrot?" Jasper that appealed to mum, that was it, that was what she had been searching for and so Jasper he became.

He stayed in the travel cage for a while before progressing to Honey's cage outside on the terrace until dad found him wandering about totally free. He was returned to the cage and dad was astonished when he promptly squeezed through the gap in the bottom of the cage and ran off again. Dad had to put some bricks around the base of the cage to stop him escaping again. Mum referred to him as a little pickle and that was his signature for the next four months except that he became a bigger and bigger pickle.

Once he was old enough, and big enough, to leave the cage Honey decided that he was her baby. From that day they regularly lie together on the sofa, Honey would wash him and they would rough and tumble together continually. It really is good to watch them both.

Personally I find him a bit of an irritant at the moment but I'm sure when he becomes an adult I will love him too.

At the moment he gets into everything and can be rather naughty, if mum opens a cupboard in the kitchen he is into it in a flash, similarly wardrobes, boxes, shopping, knitting, you name it he is into it. Despite this mum adores him which in itself is not surprising knowing mum.

Jasper is now the proud owner of his very own passport so when we all travel back to Inglan again this autumn there will, once more, be seven of us, just as it should be, and we are all really happy together.

So there you have it, my big happy family, just as I had hoped all those years ago when I was in the shed. I often think about those that helped me on my journey, Earhole, White Tail, Paws and Boy wondering what became of them. I also close my eyes and imagine that I am sitting with Ollie once more, silly I know but that's me, I am a bit of an emotional girl. Humans don't realise just how emotional we canines can be.

I am now the senior member of the four legged family, I know Simba is older than me but she doesn't want to be the matriarch and in my humble opinion I am far better qualified for the position anyway.

And that is my story thus far. I hope that you have enjoyed your walk beside me and that you have learnt things that you never dreamt possible about us canines.

I have had an unusual, but incredibly interesting life to date, long may it continue. I've had my share of trials and tribulations, I have had my share of heartache but I believe that I have also been incredibly lucky.

I am one deliriously happy Podenco.

Printed in Poland
by Amazon Fulfillment
Poland Sp. z o.o., Wrocław